ISLAMIC BELIEFS
FOR ALL

AYATOLLAAH AL-ODHMAA SHIRAZI

Translated By:
K. Noori

In the name of Allaah, the Beneficent the Merciful.

All praise is due to Allaah the Almighty.

Allaah's peace and greetings be upon the most noble human and greatest creation Mohammad, and upon his oppressed and Ma'ssom descendants.

And Allaah's curse and punishment be upon their enemies

CONTENTS

PART I: TAWHEED (THE INDIVISIBLE ONENESS OF GOD) 3
- GOD OF THE UNIVERSE 5
- WE DO NOT KNOW... 9
- HE IS ONE 11
- HE IS ALL KNOWING 17
- HE IS OMNISCIENT AND DISCERNING 21
- HE IS OMNIPOTENT 24
- HE IS WISE 28
- HE IS WILFUL 32
- HE IS THE CREATOR 35
- NATURE AND THE INVENTORS 38
- HE IS ETERNAL 40
  - *God is Eternal and Alive* *40*
- HE IS THE FIRST AND THE LAST 44
- HE IS A COMMUNICATOR 48
- HE IS TRUTHFUL 50
- HE IS SELF-SUFFICIENT 52
- HIS GRACEFUL ATTRIBUTES 57
- HE IS BASEET 63
- HE CANNOT BE SEEN 66
- NO TIME, NO PLACE 71
- HE IS NOT SUBJECT TO CHANGE 74

PART II: JUSTICE 77
- GOD IS JUST 79
- QADHAA AND QADAR 84
- FORCE AND CHOICE 88

PART III: PROPHETHOOD 93
- THE HOLY PROPHET 95
- RELIGION AND MAN-MADE LAWS 101
- THE PROPHETS AND THE PROPHET OF ISLAM 105
- WHAT IS RELIGION? 108

- *1: Belief* *108*
- *2: Morals* *113*
- *3: Worship* *115*
- *4: Other Deeds* *120*
- THE LAST PROPHET 126
- PROOF OF PROPHETHOOD 131
- MOHAMMAD AND THE QOR'AAN 136
- QOR'AAN AND THE DIVINE SCRIPTURE 139

PART IV: IMAAMAH (THE SUCCESSORSHIP OF THE PROPHET) 143

- THE IMAAM 145
- WHO ARE THE IMAAMS? 147
- THE HISTORY OF AHL AL-BAYT 149
- WHAT QUALITIES DOES AN IMAAM POSSESS? 151
  - *The Esmah of an Imaam* *153*
  - *Why is Esmah necessary for a Prophet and an Imaam?* *154*
- WHO APPOINTS THE IMAAM 157
- THE IMAAM IN OCCULTATION 164

PART V: RESURRECTION 167

- BODY AND SOUL 169
- THE WORLD OF BARZAKH 172
- THE ETERNAL LIFE 176
- HEAVEN AND HELL 180

PART I:
TAWHEED
(THE INDIVISIBLE ONENESS OF GOD)

GOD OF THE UNIVERSE

One question that arises in the minds of most people, in particular of the younger generation, is that whether the Believers who claim that there is a God are actually speaking the truth, or whether their belief is nothing but a delusion which mankind inherited from the feeble imaginations of the pre-civilisation era.

Although the assimilation of God has been made more difficult by the Monotheists through their philosophical arguments, and by the Atheists through their corruptive and paralogical languages, the answer to this question is, in fact, very simple:

A building cannot be erected without a builder. All that is in creation could not have originated without a creator; even the small hand on a clock, however small, must have a maker. Thus, imagine the entire universe with all its grandeur that embraces the dazzling sun, the moon, the sky and the rain, the earth and the plants, its humans and creatures. They all posses a complete and organised system. Nothing can alter this system. Is it therefore conceivable to claim that the universe existed just by itself and that it had no organiser? Not ever! Never can there be a system without a regulator; no motion is without a mover; no creation exists without its creator.

Thus, the Regulator of the universe is God, its Mover is God, its Creator is God.

The holy Qor'aan refers to the creation in these noble verses:

((MOST SURELY IN THE CREATION OF THE HEAVENS AND THE EARTH, AND THE ALTERNATION OF THE NIGHT AND THE DAY, AND THE SHIPS THAT RUN IN THE SEA WITH THAT WHICH PROFITS MEN, AND THE WATER THAT ALLAAH SENDS DOWN FROM THE SKY, THEN GIVES LIFE WITH IT TO THE EARTH AFTER ITS DEATH, AND SPREADS IN IT ALL (KINDS OF) ANIMALS, AND THE CHANGING OF THE WINDS AND THE CLOUDS MADE SUBSERVIENT BETWEEN THE HEAVEN AND THE EARTH, THERE ARE SIGNS FOR A PEOPLE WHO UNDERSTAND[1].))

((ALLAAH IS HE WHO RAISED THE HEAVENS WITHOUT ANY PILLARS THAT YOU SEE, AND HE IS FIRM IN POWER AND HE MADE THE SUN AND THE MOON SUBSERVIENT (TO YOU); EACH ONE PURSUES ITS COURSE TO AN APPOINTED TIME; HE REGULATES THE AFFAIR, MAKING CLEAR THE SIGNS THAT YOU MAY BE CERTAIN OF MEETING YOUR LORD.

AND HE IT IS WHO SPREAD THE EARTH AND MADE IN IT FIRM MOUNTAINS AND RIVERS, AND OF ALL FRUITS HE HAS MADE IN IT TWO KINDS; HE MAKES THE NIGHT COVER THE DAY; MOST SURELY THERE ARE SIGNS IN THIS FOR A PEOPLE WHO REFLECT.

AND IN THE EARTH THERE ARE TRACTS SIDE BY SIDE AND GARDENS OF GRAPES AND CORN AND PALM TREES HAVING ONE ROOT AND (OTHERS) HAVING DISTINCT ROOTS - THEY ARE WATERED WITH ONE WATER, AND WE MAKE SOME OF THEM EXCEL OTHERS IN FRUIT;

---

[1] Holy Qor'aan: Soorah (Chapter) 2, Aayah (Verse) 164.

PART 1: TAWHEED

MOST SURELY THERE ARE SIGNS IN THIS FOR A PEOPLE WHO UNDERSTAND[1].)).

((ALLAAH IS HE WHO CREATED THE HEAVENS AND THE EARTH AND SENT DOWN WATER FROM THE SKY, THEN BROUGHT FORTH WITH IT FRUITS AS A SUSTENANCE FOR YOU, AND HE HAS MADE THE SHIPS SUBSERVIENT TO YOU, THAT THEY MIGHT RUN THEIR COURSE IN THE SEE BY HIS COMMAND, AND HE HAS MADE THE RIVERS SUBSERVIENT TO YOU.
AND HE HAS MADE SUBSERVIENT TO YOU THE SUN AND THE MOON PURSUING THEIR COURSES, AND HE HAS MADE SUBSERVIENT TO YOU THE NIGHT AND THE DAY.
AND HE GIVES YOU OF ALL THAT YOU ASK HIM; AND IF YOU COUNT ALLAAH'S FAVOURS, YOU WILL NOT BE ABLE TO NUMBER THEM; MOST SURELY MAN IS VERY UNJUST, VERY UNGRATEFUL[2].)).

A man asked Imaam[3] Ja'far al-Saadiq(AS)[4]:

((What proof can you give me that a creator for this universe exists?" The Imaam replied: "The creation is itself proof that a creator exists - do you not glance at a building and are certain that it has a builder, even though you have never seen him, nor have you witnessed its construction?[5])).

Abu Abdullah Daysaani once asked Imaam Ja'far al-Saadiq(AS):

---

[1] Holy Qor'aan: Soorah 13, Aayaat (Verses) 2-4.
[2] Holy Qor'aan: Soorah 14, Aayaat 32-34.
[3] Imaam has a number of meanings, one of which is 'Caliph' who is a descendent and a successor of the Holy Prophet. (Translator).
[4] *Alayhes Salaam* = Peace be upon him.
[5] Al-Ehtejaaj / al-Tabarsi = page 332.

((Show me my Maker! The Imaam pointed to an egg and replied: This egg has a hard shell, beneath which is a thin layer and beneath this layer is a substance of silver and of golden colour - from a similar egg emerges different kinds of peacocks, all with various magnificent colours - do you see a designer for this product?

Daysaani contemplated deeply and thus repented by replying: I bear witness that there is no god except Allaah. He is the One, without any partner, and I bear witness that Mohammed is His Servant and Messenger and that you have been summoned by Allaah to lead mankind towards righteousness - I shall emerge out of my ignorance[1].))

---

[1] Al-Ehtejaaj / al-Tabarsi = page 333.

WE DO NOT KNOW...

what the origin of God is.

Have you ever wondered why we do not possess the knowledge of everything?

And do you realise that our ignorance is far greater than our knowledge?

Have you ever heard that science comprises of 130 branches? Physiology is one, as is Chemistry; Mathematics is another, and Medicine, etc.... and that you (mankind) know only a little of this science? How often do you read that with the vast expansion of scientific knowledge and all its inventions, the scientists surrender to the glory of the universe and confess that their inventions are nothing compared to all that lies undiscovered, and that the World is full of science and its hidden secrets?

Have you also read that the scientists, with all their inquisition and greed (for discovery), cannot explain the nature of Soul which inhabits our bodies? Have you heard that Mind in this respect is the same as Soul?

Putting aside Mind and Soul, do you know that nobody has as yet discovered what electricity is? It enlightens our homes and performs numerous functions. Although we know how it is produced, as the scientists state, its effects are visible but its source of origin remains unknown.

As we have not discovered the nature of our Mind and Soul, which accompany us throughout our life, or that of electricity of which we take full advantage, how is it therefore permissible to ask about the "nature of God?"

The nature of God is unknown to us! Man's intellect is too inferior to apprehend the nature of God! We believe and confess to its existence because we see its signs and creations, in the same way that we are certain of electricity, but to understand the nature of God is impossible.

Do you realise that no matter how sharp our sight is, it cannot see microbes, it cannot see objects from too far a distance or, in fact, at too close a proximity, nor is it capable of seeing in the dark. Mind bears some similarity to sight, the difference being that sight detects, within its limits, palpable objects whereas Mind, within its limits, detects rationality. We cannot therefore deny the existence of an object just because it happens to be out of our sight, in the same way that it would be illogical to deny the existence of God just because our intellect cannot comprehend its nature.

Looking at a building we are certain that it has a builder, although we do not see him; when we see some footprints we know that someone has walked the same track although we never see him. Creation likewise, is proof of the existence of our Creator.

We cannot comprehend the nature of God, we cannot see Him, but through His creation we believe in Him – this is sufficient proof for us.

HE IS ONE

Does this massive universe hold one God, two, or more?

Some believe in two, others in three and there are those who believe that the universe has many Gods. The answer is very simple; and of course every Monotheist will say that God is One. Before we set out our reasons for the Oneness of God, let us first consider the claims of those who believe that there is more than one God.

The dualists claim that the Gods comprise Light and Darkness. We say that Darkness and Light are created, they cannot therefore be Gods, thus their claim is unacceptable.

The Christians claim that God is The Father, The Son and The Holy Spirit. We say that Christ was a *human being* - humans themselves are created and cannot be Gods. The Holy Spirit, if it is meant as an Angel, cannot claim to be a God - what difference is there between this Angel and the others, and what is the justification for this particular Angel to have the title of God?!

The Idolaters take their idols as God and others worship animals - we ask if it is possible for a lifeless object with no capabilities of motion, or an animal that possesses no intellect which is even less inferior than a human, to be worthy of worship?

These frivolous beliefs, as far as intellectuals are concerned, are mythological and based on nothing but superstition. They hold no value for debate or discussion, and the Holy Qor'aan has briefly presented these opinions, showing what they include of superstitions and absurdities. Saying:

> *((Surely Allaah does not forgive that anything should be associated with Him, and He forgives what is besides this to whom He pleases; and whoever associates anything with Allaah, He indeed strays off into a remote error[1].))*

> *((Say: O people! If you are in doubt as to my religion, then (know that) I do not serve those whom you serve besides Allaah, but I do serve Allaah, Who will cause you to die, and I am commanded that I should be of the believers[2].))*

> *((And Allaah has said: Take not two gods, He is only One God; so of Me alone should you be afraid[3].))*

> *((Say: O Followers of the Book! be not unduly immoderate in your religion, and do not follow the low desires of people who went astray before and led many astray and went astray from the right path[4].))*

> *"Certainly they disbelieve who say: Surely,*

---

[1] Holy Qor'aan: Soorah 4, Aayah 116.
[2] Holy Qor'aan: Soorah 10, Aayah 104.
[3] Holy Qor'aan: Soorah 16, Aayah 51.
[4] Holy Qor'aan: Soorah 5, Aayah 77.

PART 1: TAWHEED

ALLAAH - HE IS THE MESSIAH, SON OF MARYAM[1].))."

((THE MESSIAH, SON OF MARYAM IS BUT AN APOSTLE; APOSTLES BEFORE HIM HAVE INDEED PASSED AWAY; AND HIS MOTHER WAS A TRUTHFUL WOMAN; THEY BOTH USED TO EAT FOOD...[2]))."

((...SAY: WHO THEN COULD CONTROL ANYTHING AS AGAINST ALLAAH WHEN HE WISHED TO DESTROY THE MESSIAH SON OF MARYAM AND HIS MOTHER AND ALL THOSE ON EARTH?[3])).

In our answer to them we say that God is unique and is not more than One, otherwise contention and conflict would arise between them, with one God's wishes being different to the other, the universe would be in disarray thus disrupting its current order, an order so perfect and splendid that only gives proof of His Oneness.

The universal system is organised in such a continual manner that everything within it is dependent upon another - had there been no water plantation would not exist, without plants no animal could live and if plants and animals were non existent mankind could not dwell. Without the Sun no being could survive, without Air the existence of any creature would be impossible (be it man, animal or plantation), to such an extent that scientists state that the being of Mankind is totally dependent upon the delicate feathers of birds without which they would be unable to fly, thus allowing reptiles and insects to destroy plantation and crops, effecting dairies and consumables, hence Mankind could not survive... This skilful monotony is the work of no other but the One God.

---

[1] Holy Qor'aan: Soorah 5, Aayah 17.
[2] Holy Qor'aan: Soorah 5, Aayah 75.
[3] Holy Qor'aan: Soorah 5, Aayah 17.

Had another existed, it *had* to make evident its power, and since this is unknown to us, the universe therefore holds no second God. The holy Qor'aan says:

> ((NEVER DID ALLAAH TAKE TO HIMSELF A SON, AND NEVER WAS THERE WITH HIM ANY (OTHER) GOD-IN THAT CASE WOULD EACH GOD HAVE CERTAINLY TAKEN AWAY WHAT HE CREATED, AND SOME OF THEM WOULD CERTAINLY HAVE OVERPOWERED OTHERS; GLORY BE TO ALLAAH ABOVE WHAT THEY DESCRIBE![1])).

> ((IF THERE HAD BEEN IN THEM ANY GODS EXCEPT ALLAAH, THEY WOULD BOTH HAVE CERTAINLY BEEN IN A STATE OF DISORDER; THEREFORE GLORY BE TO ALLAAH, THE LORD OF THE DOMINION, ABOVE WHAT THEY ATTRIBUTE (TO HIM)[2].)).

> ((SAY: PRAISE BE TO ALLAAH AND PEACE ON HIS SERVANTS WHOM HE HAS CHOSEN: IS ALLAAH BETTER, OR WHAT THEY ASSOCIATE (WITH HIM)?
> NAY, HE WHO CREATED THE HEAVENS AND THE EARTH, AND SENT DOWN FOR YOU WATER FROM THE SKY; THEN WE CAUSE TO GROW THEREBY BEAUTIFUL GARDENS; IT IS NOT POSSIBLE FOR YOU THAT YOU SHOULD MAKE THE TREES THEREOF TO GROW. IS THERE A GOD WITH ALLAAH? NAY! THEY ARE PEOPLE WHO DEVIATE.
> OR, WHO MADE THE EARTH A RESTING PLACE, AND MADE IN IT RIVERS, AND RAISED ON IT MOUNTAINS, AND PLACED BETWEEN THE TWO SEAS BARRIER. IS THERE A GOD WITH ALLAAH? NAY! MOST OF THEM DO NOT KNOW!
> OR, WHO ANSWERS THE DISTRESSED ONE WHEN HE CALLS UP ON HIM AND REMOVES THE EVIL, AND HE

---

[1] Holy Qor'aan: Soorah 23, Aayah 91.
[2] Holy Qor'aan: Soorah 21, Aayah 22.

WILL MAKE YOU SUCCESSORS IN THE EARTH. IS THERE A GOD WITH ALLAAH? LITTLE IS IT THAT YOU MIND!
OR, WHO GUIDES YOU IN UTTER DARKNESS OF THE LAND AND THE SEA, AND WHO SENDS THE WINDS AS GOOD NEWS BEFORE HIS MERCY. IS THERE A GOD WITH ALLAAH? EXALTED BY ALLAAH ABOVE WHAT THEY ASSOCIATE (WITH HIM).
OR, WHO ORIGINATES THE CREATION, THEN REPRODUCES IT, AND WHO GIVES YOU SUSTENANCE FROM THE HEAVEN AND THE EARTH. IS THERE A GOD WITH ALLAAH? SAY: BRING YOUR PROOF IF YOU ARE TRUTHFUL[1].)).

A man once asked Imaam Ja'far al-Saadiq[(AS)]:

((Why is it not possible for the Creator of the universe to be more than one? The Imaam replied: The fact that you claim God is two can be that they both have always been in existence and are powerful; or that they are both incapable; or that one is more powerful than the other. If both have the power, why does one not compete with the other so that He can be the only God? If one is powerful and the other is not, it is obvious that God is one and that is the Powerful One. As we witness the perfect organisation of the universe, the circulation of earth, the passing of day and night with the rising and setting of the sun and the moon, we have an absolute reason that its regulator is One[2].)).

With his delicate reasoning, Imaam Redhaa[(AS)] convinced a person, who believed in dualism, of the existence

---

[1] Holy Qor'aan: Soorah 27, Aayaat 59-64.
[2] Al-Ehtejaaj / al-Tabarsi = page 333.

of the one God. The Imaam replied:

> *((To say that God is two is itself proof that He is One because until you have proof of the first, you cannot pursue the second. In the first, we both believe, in the second we disagree[1].))*

Ameer al-Mo'meneen[2](AS) stated in a testament to his son, Imaam Hosayn(AS), (or Mohammad Ibn Hanafeyyah according to other narrations):

> *((Know this my son! Had your Lord another partner, the Prophets would have come to you and brought you forth proof of Its existence so that you could witness for yourself, but as Allaah has Himself acclaimed, He has no partner[3].))*

---

[1] Al-Tawheed / al-Sadooq = page 269.
[2] A title given to Imaam Ali, the first Caliph, by Allaah. It means: Commander of the Faithful. (Translator).
[3] Tohaf al-Oqool / al-Harraani, page 72.

HE IS ALL KNOWING

Allaah has the knowledge of all things, from the exact number of grains of sand and drops of water in the sea to all that lies secret within our hearts. He knows of the past and all that is to come in the future. He is incapable of making errors and His knowledge bears no difference between matters being important or immaterial.

His knowledge had pre-existed and shall remain through to eternity. His wisdom gives way to neither ignorance nor negligence. He is aware of all motions: of the mouth before its utterance, the heart beating, the limbs moving, the eyes visualising, and of all the senses be they gentle or harsh.

His wisdom and perfection is justified by the creation of all the magnificent beings that the universe holds. The existence of all the beautiful and astonishing creations become possible *only* with His knowledge and perception.

The maker of a grand towering building can only be a wise and talented person; the designer of an engine cannot be anything other than an expert and a chemist cannot produce a curable drug without his science. Could it therefore be possible for the Creator of Man, who possesses such wonderful strengths, and of creatures that have complex forms and qualities, and all other amazing beings, to be ignorant? This can never be.

The holy Qor'aan tells us:

((Do you not see that Allaah knows whatever is in the heavens and whatever is in the earth? Nowhere is there a secret counsel between three persons but He is the fourth of them, nor (between) five but He is the sixth of them, nor less than that nor more but He is with them wheresoever they are; then He will inform them of what they did on the day of Resurrection: Surely Allaah is Cognisant of all things[1].))

((And conceal your word or manifest it; surely He is Cognisant of what is in the hearts[2].))

((And with Him are the keys of the unseen treasurers - none knows them but He; and He knows what is in the land and the sea; and there falls not a leaf but He knows it, nor a grain in the darkness of the earth, nor anything green nor dry but (it is all) in a clear book.
And He it is Who takes your souls at night (in sleep), and He knows what you acquire in the day[3].))

((And you are not (engaged) in any affair, nor do you recite concerning it any portion of the Qor'aan, nor do you do any work but We are witnesses over you when you enter into it, and there does not lie concealed from your Lord

---

[1] Holy Qor'aan: Soorah 58, Aayah 7.
[2] Holy Qor'aan: Soorah 67, Aayah 13.
[3] Holy Qor'aan: Soorah 6, Aayaat 59-60.

PART 1: TAWHEED

THE WEIGHT OF A SMALL ANT IN THE EARTH OR IN THE HEAVEN, NOR ANY THING LESS THAN THAT NOR GREATER, BUT IT IS IN A CLEAR BOOK[1].))

((ALLAAH KNOWS WHAT EVERY FEMALE BEARS, AND THAT OF WHICH THE WOMBS FALL SHORT OF COMPLETION AND THAT IN WHICH THEY INCREASE; AND THERE IS A MEASURE WITH HIM OF EVERYTHING.
THE KNOWER OF THE UNSEEN AND THE SEEN, THE GREAT, THE MOST HIGH.
ALIKE (TO HIM) AMONG YOU IS HE WHO CONCEALS (HIS) WORDS AND HE WHO SPEAKS THEM OPENLY, AND HE WHO HIDES HIMSELF BY NIGHT AND (WHO) GOES FORTH BY DAY[2].))

In the words of Ameer al-Mo'meneen[AS]:

((Allaah is aware of the sounds of animals in the wilderness, of the disobedience of his Mankind, of the passing of the whales within the deep seas and of the waves that pound as the wind blows[3].))

Abu Haazem asked Imaam Ja'far al-Saadiq[AS]:

((Is it not that Allaah has full knowledge of all that has taken place and of all that is yet to come until the Resurrection? The Imaam confirmed: Even before He created the skies and the earth Allaah knew all things[4].))

Imaam Redhaa[AS] stated:

---

[1] Holy Qor'aan: Soorah 10, Aayah 61.
[2] Holy Qor'aan: Soorah 13, Aayaat 8-10.
[3] Nahj al-Balaaghah = Speech 198.
[4] Al-Tawheed / al-Sadooq = page 135.

((The Divine Knowledge exceeds all else. His knowledge pre-existed before the world had existed. He created all creatures but He knew of them before their existence. Our Lord is Grand and His power is Glorious. He is as He is of His own will, our Lord is All Knowing, All Hearing and All Seeing[1].))

---

[1] Oyoon Akhbaar al-Redhaa / al-Sadooq = vol. 1, page 118. Al-Tawheed / al-Sadooq = page 136.

HE IS OMNISCIENT AND DISCERNING

Never can people begin to converse unless Allaah has already heard them. He knows of their words even before they are uttered, whether they are spoken from the depth of the earth or the height of the skies.

There is no motion or sound, be it the rustling of leaves, the melodies of the birds, the doors closing, drums beating, thunder roaring… that our Great Lord cannot hear, even if they are the faintest of sounds that no other can hear.

God is able to see all things that are minute or grand, ugly or beautiful, moving or still, in darkness or in daylight. He can watch over His beings whether they are visible or concealed. God therefore, hears and sees all. He has total control of all sounds and of all His creation. As the holy Qor'aan says:

> *((Or do they think that We do not hear what they conceal and their secret discourses? Aye! and our messengers with them write down[1].))*.

> *((Allaah indeed knows the plea of her who pleads with you about her husband and complains to*

---
[1] Holy Qor'aan: Soorah 43, Aayah 80.

Allaah, and Allaah knows the contentions of both of you; surely Allaah is Hearing, Seeing¹.)).

((Allaah does not love the public utterance of hurtful speech, unless (it be) by one to whom injustice has been done; and Allaah is Hearing, Knowing².)).

((...To Him are (known) the unseen things of the heavens and the earth; how clear His sight and how clear His hearing! There is none to be a guardian for them besides Him, and He does not make any one His associate in His Judgment³.)).

((...Know that Allaah sees what you do⁴.)).

Imaam Redhaa^(AS) stated:

((Allaah, of His own will, has been from pre-existence Wise, Able, Abounding, Hearing and Seeing. (Although Allaah's senses are not like those of mankind and other beings)⁵.)).

Allaah is all hearing but not by using His senses, He can see everything but without sight. Had He depended upon his senses like us, He would have had to rely on them whereas Allaah is not in need of anything or anyone, otherwise He would have been composed of substances and Allaah is not a substance.

A man by the name of Abaan presented himself to

---

[1] Holy Qor'aan: Soorah 58, Aayah 1.
[2] Holy Qor'aan: Soorah 4, Aayah 148.
[3] Holy Qor'aan: Soorah 18, Aayah 26.
[4] Holy Qor'aan: Soorah 2, Aayah 233.
[5] Oyoon Akhbaar al-Redhaa / al-Sadooq = vol. 1, page 119. Al-Amaali / al-Sadooq = page 278.

PART 1: TAWHEED

Imaam Ja'far al Saadiq[AS] and asked him:

((Is Allaah always hearing, seeing, powerful and wise? The Imaam replied in the affirmative. Abaan then said to the Imaam: Someone, who claims to be one of the followers of the Ahl al-Bayt[1] claims that Allaah hears through his ears, sees with his eyes, has gained his knowledge through education and is powerful through his strength. On hearing this, the Imaam seemed displeased and replied: Whomsoever claims such a thing and believes as such is an Atheist and is not considered our follower. Allaah is powerful, He sees all and hears all of his own accord[2].))

Imaam Redhaa[AS] also said:

((Allaah has the power to hear and see everything at His own will, without the use of any faculties[3].))

---

[1] The descendants and successors of Rasoolollaah. (Translator).
[2] Al-Amaali / al-Sadooq = page 610. Al-Tawheed / al-Sadooq = page 143.
[3] Al-Tawheed / al-Sadooq = page 144.

HE IS OMNIPOTENT

Have you ever witnessed the sun rising in the east and setting in the west?

Have you ever glanced at the vegetation to see how gradually it grows, blossoms, flowers, gives fruit and then withers?

Do you see how the waves move, roar, roll and then circle?

Have you ever seen an animal produce sperm that turns into a living being which gradually forms flesh, restructures bones and then with an active heart, a well proportioned body with all its faculties and senses, steps out into the world?

Do you see the different races of humanity, the variety of mineral mines, flowing rivers, and their fishes, sparkling stars, scattered clouds, the illuminating light, the vicious thunder, etc?

Do you not notice how a plane flies? How fast a train travels and how a ship streams and glides through the ocean, breaking open the waters? And how a car twists around the roads to reach such far destinations?

All these that you see are fueled by the Divine Power!

This Divine Power has spread Its wings over all

creation and through Its grace and endless powers every being within Its universe becomes alive. His powers stretches far beyond all that is in existence - to the unknown. Not only does He dominate all within this universe but also all that has not yet been created.

How can it be so? Whilst a simple car or a piece of machinery bear evidence to the strength of its maker, does this universe therefore, with all its amazing beings, not give testimony to the immense powers of its glorious creator? The holy Qor'aan speaks of the Divine Power in such words:

((He said: I know that Allaah has power over all things[1].))

((...And Allaah is not such that anything in the heavens or in the earth should escape Him; surely He is Knowing, Powerful[2].))

((...And Allaah is the holder of power over all things[3].))

((If He pleases, He can make you pass away, O people! And bring others; and Allaah has the power to do this[4].))

It has been narrated from Imaam Saadiq(AS) who said:

((Whoever regards Allaah in the same way as he regards His creation has no religion, and whoever denies the Divine Powers is a Kaafir

---

[1] Holy Qor'aan: Soorah 2, Aayah 259.
[2] Holy Qor'aan: Soorah 35, Aayah 44.
[3] Holy Qor'aan: Soorah 18, Aayah 45.
[4] Holy Qor'aan: Soorah 4, Aayah 133.

(Atheist)[1].)).

Also it has been narrated from Imaam Baaqir who said:

((Allaah can not be described; how can He be described when He says in His book: "AND THEY DO NOT ASSIGN TO ALLAAH THE ATTRIBUTES DUE TO HIM[2]". Thus He would be greater than whatever He is described as[3].)).

Allaah's strength, as is evident, is immense to such an extent that it covers six million tiny microbes in one drop of water, and the sun which is many times larger than the earth. The Divine Power is endless and has no limits. This immense power, however, does not mean that God performs irrationally in such a way that would exceed our intellectual capacity, or demonstrate His powers in ways we cannot comprehend otherwise some would question God's abilities and doubt His powers.

Ameer al-Mo'meneen[AS] clarified this in response to someone who asked him:

((Is your Creator capable of putting the universe inside an egg, without either making the universe smaller or the egg bigger? The Imaam replied: There is nothing that our Creator cannot do, disability is not attributed to Him, but what you ask is not practical[4].)).

As anything that is not possible has no potential to

---

[1] Al-Tawheed / al-Sadooq = page 76.
[2] Holy Qor'aan: Soorah 6, Aayah 91.
[3] Al-Tawheed / al-Sadooq = page 127. Al-Mo'men = page 30.
[4] Behaar al-Anwaar / al-Majlesi = vol. 4, page 143.

exist, in the same way that a small dish cannot exceed its volume to hold more than its capacity.

HE IS WISE

The Wise and the Learned is one who does not take any action that is not deemed proper.

God performs in a wisely manner and His actions have a motive, He does not create without a reason and everything He does has a purpose.

Wisdom is like a belt that beholds other attributes of God. Had it not been for Wisdom, Power would have created many useless things. Mankind would be unjustly dealt with by being either rewarded or punished unfairly, there would have been no balance in their daily sustenance, and our lands would have dried up beyond control, etc...

It is because of God's Wisdom that the standard of His qualities is justly and equally spread over the creation, and it is as a result of His wisdom that everything within this universe has a reason for existence. It is according to His wisdom that plants do not grow overnight, conception does not take place in the open, children do not develop intellect within an hour - everything happens according to plan, in an orderly manner, although the Divine Power is extensive and capable of anything.

However, man's intellect and knowledge is limited to be able to comprehend this Divine Wisdom and the universal science. There are times when we wonder at some of the creation and question whether their existence is really necessary but if we carefully focus on them, we become aware of the reasons for their existence. This is why we should accept that everything is created according to the Divine Knowledge and His reasoning, even though we are not able to understand them.

When we look at a plane, for example, we notice that all its various parts are orderly placed and set out but we may not know what each of the tools or screws are used for. The fault, therefore, lies with us for not having this knowledge and not with the plane. The holy Qor'aan refers to the Divine Wisdom in the following verses:

> *((...(THIS IS) A BOOK, WHOSE VERSES ARE MADE DECISIVE, THEN ARE THEY MADE PLAIN, FROM THE WISE, ALL-AWARE[1].))*.

> *((AND MOST SURELY YOU ARE MADE TO RECEIVE THE QOR'AAN FROM THE WISE, THE KNOWING GOD[2].))*.

> *((FALSEHOOD SHALL NOT COME TO IT, FROM BEFORE IT NOR FROM BEHIND IT, A REVELATION FROM THE WISE, THE PRAISED ONE[3].))*.

> *((YA SEEN - I SWEAR BY THE QOR'AAN FULL OF WISDOM[4].))*.

In a famous narration from Imaam Ja'far al-Saadiq[AS], known as "Tawheed al-Mofadhal", the Imaam describes to

---

[1] Holy Qor'aan: Soorah 11, Aayah 1.
[2] Holy Qor'aan: Soorah 27, Aayah 6.
[3] Holy Qor'aan: Soorah 41, Aayah 42.
[4] Holy Qor'aan: Soorah 36, Aayah 1.

Mofadhal[1] some of the signs of the Divine Wisdom. This narration is lengthy, so we mention here only a small extract from it:

> *((Mofadhal! First, we begin with the creation of Mankind.*
> *The initial foundation to be laid for the creation of Mankind is the foetus in the mother's womb. This foetus, which is confined within three covers, begins to feel the revolutionary touch of the Divine Powers. These three covers are the stomach bag, the womb and the birth bag.*
> *Because of this confinement, the foetus does not have the strength to provide food for itself, neither can it defend nor harm itself. Hence, the menses (menstrual discharge from the mother's womb) become its daily food, just as water is food to plants.*
> *This blood is a constant feed for the baby until its growth becomes complete; its body gains strength and develops layers of skin that is able to tolerate the external air. Its eyes begin to gain sight and suddenly, the contractions begin and the labour pains thus cause the mother to give birth.*
> *As soon as the baby is born, the same blood that was once its food whilst in the womb, works its way up to the mother's breasts, its colour and taste begin to change and becomes a different food altogether (milk) which now becomes a more suitable food for the baby than blood and is always ready for whenever the baby requires it.*
> *The moment the baby is born, it demands food by feeling and moving its lips and the moment it sees the breasts the baby knows to feed milk*

---

[1] One of the Imaam's students who was himself a scholar. (Translator).

from them and uses this milk for as long as its body is moist and fresh, its lungs are thin and its limbs are fragile, until it starts to walk - by which time, it then requires a more nourishing food so that it can fully develop its strength. At the same time, it starts to grow teeth in order to be able to chew this food...[1])).

---

[1] Tawheed al-Mofadhal = page 48.

HE IS WILFUL

Will is opposed by coercion.

The fire burns but its burning is without its will. And a human being walks but his walk is according to his will.

God performs according to, and based on, His own will and power. He chooses to create Mankind and so He does, He brings ailments on whomever he chooses, it is His intention for plants to grow and so they do. That is to say, whatever is within the universe has been created by God's will - in any form or shape and in whatever time and place that He desires it to be. There is no other who can match His will and He is totally indispensable.

God has the power and is able to shape the embryo in the mother's womb into a male or a female or He can take the strength and weaken a strong person. All that He has created now, He can also create in another era - whatever has been created in one place He can duplicate it in another.

The fact that He can create a being in one particular shape and not in any other; or in one certain place rather than elsewhere; or in a specific period than in any other time is itself proof that God possesses immense will and power that places the entire universe under His authority and He can therefore do with His creation as He wishes and in whichever

PART 1: TAWHEED   33

form He so desires.
The holy Qor'aan elaborates on this point in its following verses:

> *((IF HE PLEASES, HE CAN MAKE YOU PASS AWAY, O PEOPLE! AND BRING OTHERS; AND ALLAAH HAS THE POWER TO DO THIS[1].))*.

> *((DO YOU NOT SEE THAT ALLAAH CREATED THE HEAVENS AND THE EARTH WITH TRUTH? IF HE PLEASES HE WILL TAKE YOU OFF AND BRING A NEW CREATION[2].))*.

> *((OUR WORD FOR A THING WHEN WE INTEND IT, IS ONLY THAT WE SAY TO IT, BE, AND IT IS[3].))*.

> *((SAY: WHO IS IT THAT CAN WITHHOLD YOU FROM ALLAAH IF HE INTENDS TO DO YOU EVIL, RATHER HE INTENDS TO SHOW YOU MERCY? AND THEY WILL NOT FIND FOR THEMSELVES BESIDES ALLAAH ANY GUARDIAN OR HELPER[4].))*.

It has been narrated from Imaam Saadiq who said:

((Allaah created the things with Mashee'ah[5].)).

And he was asked:

((Has Allaah always had a will?
Imaam Saadiq answered: There is will when there is something to be done. Allaah was

---

[1] Holy Qor'aan: Soorah 4, Aayah 133.
[2] Holy Qor'aan: Soorah 14, Aayah 19.
[3] Holy Qor'aan: Soorah 16, Aayah 40.
[4] Holy Qor'aan: Soorah 33, Aayah 17.
[5] Behaar al-Anwaar / al-Majlesi = vol. 4, page 145.

always All-Knowing and All-Powerful, and then he willed?[1]*))*.

Allaah is wise and able, He can therefore do as he chooses. When He intends for something to be, it is done... As He also expects good deed's from His servants and despises their wrong doings.

The holy Qor'aan further says:

((...ALLAAH DESIRES EASE FOR YOU, AND HE DOES NOT DESIRE FOR YOU DIFFICULTY[2].*))*.

Imaam Redhaa[AS] stated:

((Allaah's will and desire with respect to worship is: His order to obey and His help and satisfaction in so doing; and His will and desire with respect to evil deeds is: aversion from them and His anger and discontent if we don't.
Then a man asked: Does this therefore, mean that Allaah can rule over His servant's deeds? The Imaam replied: Indeed! His servants cannot do anything good or bad unless Allaah is ruling over such deeds. He further replied: This means that Allaah judges over His servants and passes on to them what they are entitled to: rewards for their good deeds and punishment for their bad deeds - in this world and in the Hereafter[3].*))*.

---

[1] Al-Kaafi / al-Kolayni = vol. 1, page 109.
[2] Holy Qor'aan: Soorah 2, Aayah 185.
[3] Behaar al-Anwaar / al-Majlesi = vol. 5, page 11.

HE IS THE CREATOR

God is the Creator of all things. For every molecule there is yet a smaller one; for every creation there is yet one which is more grand. All are created by no other but God. He has no partner and requires no help in creating - nor does He seek assistance in its formation.

It is He who has created the sun and the moon, the plants and the animals, the sky and the earth, and it is He who has created Mankind and given it superiority over other Beings.

In the production of offspring, Man is only a "vehicle". His only role is the intercourse with his partner. However, the transfer of the sperm from the father into the mother's womb, its stability, its growth, its formation of bones, veins, eyes, ears, mouth, the breathing of soul into its body, its different forms and shapes, etc. are all the magnanimous works of God!

A farmer ploughs, sows and waters, but the growing of the plant, its blossoming, its fruit, its production, etc. are from God. All that we see in the universe: large or small, plants and minerals, humans and animals, solids and liquids, dead or alive are the creations of God. The holy Qor'aan says:

> ((WHO MADE THE EARTH A RESTING PLACE FOR YOU AND THE HEAVEN A CANOPY AND (WHO) SENDS DOWN RAIN FROM THE SKY, THEN BRINGS FORTH WITH IT SUBSISTENCE FOR YOU OF THE FRUITS; THEREFORE DO NOT SET UP RIVALS TO ALLAAH WHILE YOU KNOW[1].)).

> ((HE CREATED MAN FROM A SMALL SEED AND LO! HE IS AN OPEN CONTENDER.

---

[1] Holy Qor'aan: Soorah 2, Aayah 22.

AND HE CREATED THE CATTLE FOR YOU; YOU HAVE IN THEM WARM CLOTHING AND (MANY) ADVANTAGES, AND OF THEM DO YOU EAT.
AND THERE IS BEAUTY IN THEM FOR YOU WHEN YOU DRIVE THEM BACK (TO HOME), AND WHEN YOU SEND THEM FORTH (TO PASTURE)[1].))

((...AND HE CREATES WHAT YOU DO NOT KNOW[2].)).

((HE CREATED THE HEAVENS AND THE EARTH WITH THE TRUTH[3].)).

((DO THEY NOT SEE THAT WE HAVE CREATED CATTLE FOR THEM, OUT OF WHAT OUR HANDS HAVE WROUGHT, SO THEY ARE THEIR MASTERS?[4])).

((AND ALLAAH CREATED YOU OF DUST, THEN OF THE LIFE-GERM, THEN HE MADE YOU PAIRS[5].)).

((THAT IS ALLAAH, YOUR LORD, THE CREATOR OF EVERYTHING; THERE IS NO GOD BUT HE; WHENSE ARE YOU THEN TURNED AWAY?[6])).

((GLORY BE TO HIM WHO CREATED PAIRS OF ALL THINGS, OF WHAT THE EARTH GROWS AND OF THEIR KIND AND OF WHAT THEY DO NOT KNOW[7].)).

There are those who believe that God cannot possibly be the Maker of creatures such as flies and insects which are

---

[1] Holy Qor'aan: Soorah 16, Aayaat 4-6.
[2] Holy Qor'aan: Soorah 16, Aayah 8.
[3] Holy Qor'aan: Soorah 16, Aayah 3.
[4] Holy Qor'aan: Soorah 36, Aayah 71.
[5] Holy Qor'aan: Soorah 35, Aayah 11.
[6] Holy Qor'aan: Soorah 23, Aayah 62.
[7] Holy Qor'aan: Soorah 36, Aayah 36.

born in the swamps. Their belief, however, could not be further from the truth because for each creation God has also brought forth a cause for living, in the same way that He has brought about the creation of humans through a man and a woman. Likewise, for flies, insects and worms there are swamps and creeks, and for germs and bacteria there is dirt and rubbish.

A man by the name of Abu al-Awjaa' once asked Imaam Ja'far al Saadiq:

> *((Is it not so that you claim God is the Creator of all beings? After the Imaam agreed with him, he continued: I, too am capable of creating. The Imaam asked him how this was so, to which Abu al-Awjaa' replied: I will empty my excrement in a certain spot and wait until it transforms into flies. It is therefore I who have created such creatures. The Imaam replied: Is it not true that a creator knows the status of its creation? If you claim to have created these species, can you also distinguish whether they are of a male or a female gender or do you know of their life expectancy?![1]))*.

Man is used only as an instrument for making things happen. To think that he is capable of creating another being is impossible!

---

[1] Behaar al-Anwaar / al-Majlesi = vol. 3, page 50.

NATURE AND THE INVENTORS

What is nature? Can we consider this to be the 'Creator'?

A human being (who, according to you is created by nature) is a complete being who possesses eyes and ears, senses of touch and smell, has powers of intellect and gains considerable knowledge and experience.

But nature, (that you believe to be the creator of Mankind) is incomplete and possesses no power.

So what is nature? Is it the earth? The sun? The light, the heat or water? Or is it air? Or are these all a formation of nature? Or is nature an expression for the order that governs the universe?

Do you believe that the voiceless earth which neither hears nor sees, or the sun and all universal elements which, like the earth are inarticulate, can be capable of creating such a delicate, beautiful and loving thing such as the soul in the human body?

Can the rotation of the planets in such an organised manner happen just by itself?

An old wise woman used to say: "My small weaving machine needs me to spin it; is it therefore possible for this grand universe not to have a master?" These questions are worthy of consideration and should be given more thought!

One who glances at this world and believes that nature has created it and thus looks at the world as nature, is like one who glances at a building and believes that it was built by itself!

Do you therefore accept that such beliefs are correct to come from a logical and an intelligent person? Indeed, they cannot be ...

This universe boasts a God that is Wise, Able and Powerful - One that has created it and assigned to it such an impeccable order.

THE SCIENTISTS AND THE INVENTORS

These groups of people should truly be more steadfast in their faith than others because an inventor owes his superiority to the fact that he brings forth a discovery that was already in existence but was unknown to Man. It is due to his countless efforts that such an invention is exposed. However, it is the invention itself that proves it has a Creator, and after centuries of obscurity, God has caused the intellect of such a scientist as being inherent in its discovery.

Otherwise, who has formed air in such a way that it enables aircrafts to fly? Who has given steam such power that it is capable of moving ships and trains? Who has given the radar sight to detect from such a distance? Who is it that causes ether to be the bearer of sound?

HE IS ETERNAL

Life is the opposite of death and frailty. A human being has life, animals have life, plants have life in the sense that these beings are moving and active and whilst alive, are not feeble.

A living is one that signifies perfection. A human being sees, hears, comprehends, works. An animal eats, drinks, walks; a living plant grows, blossoms and fruits.

But one thing which is apparent is that the quality of life in beings differ. The life of a human being is greater than that of an animal and the life of an animal is far better than that of a plant. Likewise, the life of some people can be of a different quality than others. It can be possible, for example, that the life of one person is better than another, meaning that the greater signs of life a person has the better quality of life he will lead. This also applies to animals and plants...

GOD IS ETERNAL AND ALIVE

Although not in the sense that He consumes and grows as these relate to substances, and we have proved that God is not a substance. But in the sense that God creates, is Wise, Willing, Powerful, gives life, takes life, gives us our daily sustenance, rewards good deeds and punishes those with evil deeds. Some 'unsound' philosophers believe that God works but has no life, in the same way that a piece of automatic machinery performs. But do they not realise that this machinery is consistent and only performs the one task they are designed for and is incapable of doing anything else beyond that. God, on the other hand is constantly at work.

((ALL THOSE WHO ARE IN THE HEAVENS AND THE EARTH ASK OF HIM; EVERY MOMENT HE IS IN A STATE (OF GLORY)[1].))

We can see for ourselves that He overflows us with signs of His existence in the forms of shapes and figures, volumes and moulds, with colours and quality; not only everyday but every minute and second when one is born into this life and another departs from it, one gives birth and another is made infertile, the earth blossoms and flourishes it then dries up and withers, an infant develops into a youth and then ages. Within nature we see changes that rapidly take place, the clouds are moved from one side to the other, some are scattered in one place and after pouring down their rain they move on to be scattered elsewhere.

God is therefore alive and the reins of the entire universe is within His power, working constantly at all times. There are some who think that God resides in the skies and some believe that He is in Heaven. There are also those who think of Him as light and others imagine Him to be just like humans, with a head, face, hands and legs! These imaginations however, are far from reality and are rejected by the holy Qor'aan and traditions.

If God is residing in heaven He will be in need of it, if He had a body He would depend on it but as we had said

---

[1] Holy Qor'aan: Soorah 55, Aayah 29.

before: God, in every sense of the word, is independent and will never be in need of anything.

The Qor'aan says:

((ALLAAH IS HE BESIDES WHOM THERE IS NO GOD, THE EVERLASTING, THE SELF-SUBSISTING BY WHOM ALL SUBSIST; SLUMBER DOES NOT OVERTAKE HIM NOR DOES SLEEP; WHATEVER IS IN THE HEAVENS AND WHATEVER IS ON THE EARTH IS HIS; HE KNOWS WHAT IS BEFORE THEM AND WHAT IS BEHIND THEM...[1]))

((AND RELY ON THE EVER-LIVING WHO DIES NOT, AND CELEBRATE HIS PRAISE; AND SUFFICIENT IS HE AS BEING AWARE OF THE FAULTS OF HIS SERVANTS[2].))

((AND THE FACES SHALL BE HUMBLED BEFORE THE LIVING, THE SELF-SUBSISTENT GOD, AND HE WHO BEARS INIQUITY IS INDEED A FAILURE[3].))

The signs of life within humans, however plenty, is limited and restricted within the boundaries of time and place. However, the existence of life within God, unlike humans, is unlimited. Neither time nor place can set Him any limitations. Everything that is within this wide universe is a sign of His existence to such an extent that our life seems a tiny speck compared to God's.

The Jews were of the belief that God does not perform any tasks and after having created the universe He withdrew and went into a period of rest. But God attacks their denials in the holy Qor'aan:

---

[1] Holy Qor'aan: Soorah 2, Aayah 255.
[2] Holy Qor'aan: Soorah 25, Aayah 58.
[3] Holy Qor'aan: Soorah 20, Aayah 111.

((AND THE JEWS SAY: THE HANDS OF ALLAAH ARE TIED UP! THEIR HANDS SHALL BE SHACKLED AND THEY SHALL BE CURSED FOR WHAT THEY SAY. NAY, BOTH HIS HANDS ARE SPREAD OUT, HE EXPENDS AS HE PLEASES...[1])).

---

[1] Holy Qor'aan: Soorah 5, Aayah 64.

HE IS THE FIRST AND THE LAST

Pre-existent and eternal – All that we see in the universe has to have a beginning and an end. There have been other beings; of humans, animals and plantation that lived before us and we have witnessed their existence as well as their destruction.

As for the earth, the sun, the moon, mountains, the seas, the stars and of the day and night, we have not observed their creation, and we will not live long enough to witness their termination. However, the scientists and the intellectuals tell us that "millions of years ago there was no sign of the universe" and that "the universe will exist for so many millions of years, after which time everything will be destroyed and no signs of it will remain."

The one who created the world is God and the one who would be responsible for its termination will be God. He is ahead of all things and will remain after all has been destroyed. He is a Pre-existence that nothing had existed before Him and will be an Eternity, with nothing remaining after Him.

During the period when there were no time and no place, no movement or stability, no skies and stars, no earth, water, rain, air and other beings, there was only God and after

PART 1: TAWHEED

all these, it will only be God that will remain. Therefore a time will come when the earth and the sun will no longer rotate, no seas will flow, nothing will grow, and no being can move but only God will exist. If we glance back to the past we can see that God had been in existence before all things and there will never come a time when He will not be in existence.

Should anyone claim that: "there was a time in the past that God did not exist" we will thus ask them: "in that case who was it that created God?" And should anyone further state that: "There will come a time when there will be no God", we shall ask "Who will destroy God?" These statements are therefore not factual. Hence, God is the first; He had no beginning, and He is Last; He has no end.

The holy Qor'aan tells us that:

((...IS IT NOT SUFFICIENT AS REGARDS YOUR LORD THAT HE IS A WITNESS OVER ALL THINGS?[1]))

Therefore God is the witness of all beings — of those in existence now and of those that were in the past and shall remain a witness of their destruction.

The holy Qor'aan further says:

((...AND WE ARE NOT TO BE OVERCOME[2].))

((WHATEVER IS IN THE HEAVENS AND EARTH DECLARES THE GLORY OF ALLAAH, AND HE IS THE MIGHTY, THE WISE.
HIS IS THE KINGDOM OF THE HEAVENS AND THE EARTH; HE GIVES LIFE AND CAUSES DEATH; AND HE HAS POWER OVER ALL THINGS.

---

[1] Holy Qor'aan: Soorah 41, Aayah 53.
[2] Holy Qor'aan: Soorah 56, Aayah 60.

HE IS THE FIRST AND LAST AND THE ASCENDANT (OVER ALL) AND THE KNOWER OF HIDDEN THINGS, AND HE IS COGNIZANT OF ALL THINGS[1].))

Someone by the name of Naafe' bin Azraq asked Imaam Baaqir[AS]:

((At what time there was God?. The Imaam told him: Alas! You tell me of a time when there was no God, so that I can tell you of a time when there was God! Pure is the God that has always been and will always be. He is One upon whom all depend. He does not associate for Himself any partner, or children[2].)).

It has been narrated from Imaam Saadiq who said:

*((Ra's al-Jaaloot was telling other Jews that the Moslems believe that Ali is the most well spoken and intellectual of all! Follow me and I will take you to visit him so that I can ask him certain questions which will prove him wrong.
They went to see Ameer al-Mo'meneen[AS] and Jaaloot said: I would like to ask you questions on a certain issue. The Imaam replied: Ask me whatever you wish. Jaaloot then continued: When was our Lord created? The Imaam responded: Oh Jew! This question would be in the case of one who had never exited before and was then created. Our Lord possesses an existence that has no limits. How could anything have existed before Him whilst He had always pre-existed... The ending of all things is in His*

---

[1] Holy Qor'aan: Soorah 57, Aayaat 1-3.
[2] Al-Tawheed / al-Sadooq = page 173. Behaar al-Anwaar / al-Majlesi = vol. 3, page 284.

power, and after all have perished He will thus remain...[1])).

Allaah says:

((EVERYTHING IS PERISHABLE BUT HE; HIS IS THE JUDGEMENT, AND TO HIM YOU SHALL BE BROUGHT BACK[2].)).

---

[1] Behaar al-Anwaar / al-Majlesi = vol. 3, page 286
[2] Holy Qor'aan: Soorah 28, Aayah 88.

HE IS A COMMUNICATOR

Man uses speech in order to express and expose his mental and inner self. Animals too, have each their own special noises. But God does not need to speak as He can use His will and power to Create and can, through the minds of His angels and the prophets, achieve His purpose. However, in spite of His attributes it has been known to us by the holy Qor'aan and various narrations that God speaks.

This does not mean that God possesses a tongue, lips and vocal cords, as God is not a body and unlike humans He has no organs (which we will explain later). Therefore, the Divine words are different to those of man which are uttered verbally. God speaks in the sense that whenever He wishes to do so, He will create noises either in the air or elsewhere or He may create something that can be heard by the angels, the prophets and anyone who wishes to hear it.

The holy Qor'aan says:

((...AND TO MOOSA, ALLAAH ADDRESSED HIS WORD, SPEAKING (TO HIM)[1].)).

---

[1] Holy Qor'aan: Soorah 4, Aayah 164.

The meaning of the 'Word' is meant to be the Divine graces, bounties, creations, etc. The Qor'aan further says:

((AND WERE EVERY TREE THAT IS IN THE EARTH (MADE INTO) PENS AND THE SEA (TO SUPPLY IT WITH INK), WITH SEVEN MORE SEAS TO INCREASE IT, THE WORDS OF ALLAAH WOULD NOT COME TO AN END; SURELY ALLAAH IS MIGHTY AND WISE[1].))

((SAY: IF THE SEA WERE INK FOR THE WORDS OF MY LORD, THE SEA WOULD SURELY BE CONSUMED BEFORE THE WORDS OF MY LORD ARE EXHAUSTED, THOUGH WE WERE TO BRING THE LIKE OF THAT (SEA) TO ADD THERETO[2].))

Imaam Ja'far Saadiq[AS] said:

((God had existed at the time when there were no speakers – He thus created speech[3].))

And according to Imaam Redhaa[AS]:

((The words of the Creator are not the same as the words of His creation. The Creator does not talk by the use of His mouth or the movement of the tongue[4].))

---

[1] Holy Qor'aan: Soorah 31, Aayah 27.
[2] Holy Qor'aan: Soorah 18, Aayah 109.
[3] Behaar al-Anwaar / al-Majlesi = vol. 4, page 68.
[4] Behaar al-Anwaar / al-Majlesi = vol. 4, page 152.

HE IS TRUTHFUL

God is truthful.
There are three reasons that urges one to lie:

1- A vile and impure nature
2- Being unable to accept one's own losses or defeat, unless through lies
3- Lack of information

Can there be any other reasons as to why one should behold the truth? Indeed not, as the motives for speaking lies fall within the above three categories. But God:

1- Is exempt from any impurities and possesses no indecency or vileness
2- He is Powerful, there is nothing on earth or in the heavens that can disable Him
3- God has the knowledge of all things. Regardless of its importance or insignificance, nothing had ever been unknown to Him and never will be.

Therefore, with His words God is always sincere. With the promises of His good tidings and those of His fearful punishments He will never lie and neither will he abandon His promises, nor hesitate in fulfilling them. His promises to reward the Believers with gardens and springs, green fields and resting places, beautiful homes and flowing rivers, colourful fruits and endless bounties are all true and will be fulfilled. Similarly, His promises to the Unbelievers that He will inflict upon them the most painful punishments and the fire of hell and cover them with heavy smoke, with no canopy to protect them to reduce the heat, are all true and will be fulfilled.

The holy Qor'aan refers to them:

((...THIS WAS A PUNISHMENT WE GAVE THEM ON ACCOUNT OF THEIR REBELLION, AND WE ARE SURELY TRUTHFUL[1].))

((THEN WE MADE OUR PROMISE GOOD TO THEM, SO WE DELIVERED THEM AND THOSE WHOM WE PLEASED, AND WE DESTROYED THE EXTRAVAGANT[2].))

---

[1] Holy Qor'aan: Soorah 6, Aayah 146.
[2] Holy Qor'aan: Soorah 21, Aayah 9.

HE IS SELF-SUFFICIENT

Notice how the wealthy people who have nothing in this world except money, are referred to as 'wealthy' and 'self-sufficient'. The title of 'wealthy' for these group of people is not appropriate as this person of wealth who is free from want is himself, from head to toe, totally needy because he personally has no control over life or death, profit or loss, health and ailments, youth and ageing, beauty or disability. The only thing is that his impoverished friend does not have the money that he has.

But when we claim that God is wealthy, it means that He is Self-sufficient in every sense:

* In his existence: He needs no one to create Him
* In His rulership: He needs no one to pass Him the power
* In His knowledge and wisdom: He needs no trainer or teacher
* In His management of the creation: He needs no help, minister or aid
* In His essence: He needs no instrument or experience

It should be known that the reason for God's wealth is not because He owns valuable mines, or that He is the King of the Jinn, the Angels and the humans, and not because He is the owner of this boundless universe with all its water and land, and not because He owns the treasures and the wealth of the people such as water and air, light and earth, from which the trees give fruit, the plants grow and the animals are created, no! The wealth of God is not because of having all this; the secret of the His wealth lies in that grand and matchless Power that can create whatever He wants and destroy whatever He wishes, that unparalleled Power, the endless treasure and the mystery of His wealth lies in the word 'Be' – whenever He intends to, He can create many worlds and galaxies with only a signal and willpower, without the slightest trouble or difficulty. The holy Qor'aan says:

((HIS COMMAND, WHEN HE INTENDS ANYTHING, IS ONLY TO SAY TO IT: BE, SO IT IS[1].))

And those hypocrites had foolish ideas as the holy Qor'aan repeats their claim:

((THEY (THE HYPOCRITES) IT IS WHO SAY: DO NOT SPEND UPON THOSE WHO ARE WITH THE APOSTLE OF ALLAAH UNTIL THEY BREAK UP[2].)). (63:7)

They believed that the Holy Prophet desperately needed their help, and without their financial help the Moslems would desert the Prophet and that God could not save them from poverty. But God sent them this reply:

---

[1] Holy Qor'aan: Soorah 36, Aayah 82.
[2] Holy Qor'aan: Soorah 63, Aayah 7.

((... AND ALLAAH'S ARE THE TREASURES OF THE HEAVENS AND THE EARTH, BUT THE HYPOCRITES DO NOT UNDERSTAND[1].))

Without a doubt, knowledge, creation, sustenance, death, resurrection, health, illness, wealth, status... all lay within the enormous Divine treasures, He will give to whomsoever He wishes and will take from whomsoever He wishes. As God says:

((AND THERE IS NOT A THING BUT WITH US ARE THE TREASURES OF IT, AND WE DO NOT SEND IT DOWN BUT IN A KNOWN MEASURE[2].))

The moment this blessed verse was revealed: *((WHO IS IT THAT WILL OFFER TO ALLAAH A GOODLY GIFT, SO HE WILL MULTIPLY IT TO HIM MANIFOLD...[3]))*, a group of Jews mockingly claimed that: "The God of Mohammad has become poor and we are wealthy".

They believed that their wealth had made them free from need and thought that this verse was proof of God's need and poverty. For this reason God sent them a reply in another verse in which He threatens them with punishment:

((ALLAAH HAS CERTAINLY HEARD THE SAYING OF THOSE WHO SAID: SURELY ALLAAH IS POOR AND WE ARE RICH. I WILL RECORD WHAT THEY SAY, AND THEIR KILLING THE PROPHETS UNJUSTLY, AND I WILL SAY: TASTE THE CHASTISEMENT OF BURNING.

---

[1] Holy Qor'aan: Soorah 63, Aayah 7.
[2] Holy Qor'aan: Soorah 15, Aayah 21.
[3] Holy Qor'aan: Soorah 2, Aayah 245.

PART 1: TAWHEED   55

> *This is for what your own hands have sent before and because Allaah is not in the least unjust to the servants[1].))*

Another group of people believe that God is in need of their faith, but neither the faith of the faithful is of any benefit to God nor is the denial of the non-believers of any harm to Him. He is totally free from needing anything. The benefits of having faith will be given to the believers and the detriment of denial will be for the non-believers.

The holy Qor'aan quotes Moosa:

> *((And Moosa said: If you are ungrateful, you and those on earth all together, most surely Allaah is Self-sufficient, Praised[2].))*

In another verse the holy Qor'aan says:

> *((And whoever strives hard, he strives only for his own soul; most surely Allaah is Self-sufficient, above (need of) the worlds[3].))*

In another verse God refers to those people who turned away from the teachings of the Prophets and deviated towards the path of the non-believers:

> *((Has there not come to you the story of those who disbelieved before, then tasted the evil result of their conduct, and they had a painful punishment?*
> *That is because there came to them their apostles with clear arguments, but they said:*

---
[1] Holy Qor'aan: Soorah 3, Aayaat 181-182.
[2] Holy Qor'aan: Soorah 14, Aayah 8.
[3] Holy Qor'aan: Soorah 29, Aayah 6.

SHALL MORTALS GUIDE US? SO THEY DISBELIEVED AND TURNED BACK, AND ALLAAH DOES NOT STAND IN NEED (OF ANYTHING), AND ALLAAH IS SELF-SUFFICIENT, PRAISED[1].))

If anyone was to state that: "God does not need my obedience so why should I put myself through the trouble and worship Him?" or if they say that: "God does not need my wealth so why should I give in the way of God?" they are being illogical because the rewards of obeying God and helping the poor will be given to themselves, and will become beneficial for the society and for themselves.

If a student was to say that: "The government does not need me to succeed in my exams and does not lose out if I were to fail, so why should I then go through the trouble of staying awake all night to study?" Of course, the intellectuals consider those who think the same as this student as ignorant. Although their success or failure is immaterial to the government, this sort of mentality is refuted.

And as we know the government is less wealthy and powerful that God; so would it make any sense for someone to say: "why should I put myself through the difficulty of obeying God, when He does not need it?"

---

[1] Holy Qor'aan: Soorah 64, Aayaat 5-6.

HIS GRACEFUL ATTRIBUTES

God is so grand that He cannot be restricted to any phase, place or cause. His attributes are unlimited and He possesses enormous virtues that are endless:

1- To describe the extent of His qualities: The Divine wisdom and knowledge are not limited so one cannot claim that "God knows one particular thing and not another", or that "God has the power over certain things but is incapable of others" or "He can hear a certain voice but cannot hear all." These restrictions relate only to Man and other creations.
2- To describe His qualities in numbers: The qualities attributed to God are enormous and whatever has been described of the Divine attributes so far, such as knowledge, power, life, determination... are but a small number of the Divine qualities. A number of these qualities have been mentioned in the holy Qor'aan and in a number of narrations, a few of which we will list in this section.

The holy Qor'aan says:

((He is the Allaah, besides Whom there is no god; the Knower of the unseen and the seen; He is the Beneficent, the Merciful.
He is Allaah, besides Whom there is no god; the King, the Holy, the Giver of peace, the Granter of security, Guardian over all, the Mighty, the Supreme, the Possessor of every greatness; Glory be to Allaah from what they set up (with Him).
He is Allaah the Creator, the Maker, the Fashioner; His are the most excellent names; whatever is in the heavens and the earth declares His glory; and He is The Mighty, the Wise[1].))

Imaam Ja'far al Saadiq[AS] narrated from his father, Mohammed Ibn Ali, and he from his fathers that the Prophet of God had said:

((There are 99 names of God, 100 except one, whoever calls out these names Heaven will be rewarded to him. The names are:[2]

No	Holy Name	Meaning
1	Allaah	The One God
2	Ilaah	The One
3	Al-Waahid	The Undividable One
4	Al-Ahad	The One and Only
5	Al-Samad	The Eternal One
6	Al-Awwal	The First

---

[1] Holy Qor'aan: Soorah 59, Aayaat 22-24.
[2] Al-Khesaal / al-Sadooq = page 593. Al-Tawheed / al-Sadooq = page 219.

7	Al-Aakhir	The Last
8	Al-Samee'	The All-Hearing of what is said and thought
9	Al-Basseer	The All-Seeing of what is seen and what is not
10	Al-Qadeer	The Omnipotent
11	Al-Qaahir	The Conqueror (with death) of all
12	Al-Ali	The Exalted
13	Al-A'laa	The Most High
14	Al-Baaqee	The Eternal
15	Al-Badee'	The Initiator of all creation
16	Al-Baare'	The Creator of all creation
17	Al-Akram	The Most Noble
18	Al-Dhaahir	The Manifest (in His evidences and facts)
19	Al-Baatin	The Concealed (beyond mind comprehension)
20	Al-Hayy	The Ever-Living
21	Al-Hakeem	The Wise
22	Al-Hafeedh	The Preserver of existence
23	Al-Haqq	The Truthful, the Ultimate Truth
24	Al-Haseeb	The Reckoner
25	Al-Hameed	The All-Praised and Ultimate Praiseworthy
26	Al-Khafii	The Mysterious
27	Al-Rabb	The Lord
28	Al-Rahmaan	The most Merciful to all creation
29	Al-Raheem	The most Compassionate to His believers
30	Al-Thaari'	The Protector
31	Al-Razzaaq	The Provider
32	Al-Raqeeb	The Watchful Supervisor
33	Al-Ra'oof	The Merciful and Compassionate

34	Al-Haleem	The Forbearant
35	Al-Salaam	The Peaceful One
36	Al-Mu'min	The Faithful to His worshipers
37	Al-Muhaimin	The Ever-present witness to all His subject's deeds
38	Al-Azeez	The Respected and Triumphant over all
39	Al-Jabbaar	The Almighty One
40	Al-Mutakabbir	The Proud One
41	Al-Sanad	The Supporter
42	Al-Subbooh	The Glorified One
43	Al-Shaheed	The Witness to all
44	Al-Saadiq	The Truthful One
45	Al-Saani'	The Maker of everything
46	Al-Taahir	The Pure
47	Al-Adl	The Just, The Equitable
48	Al-Afoww	The Pardoning, The Forgiver
49	Al-Ghafoor	The Most Forgiving
50	Al-Ghani	The All-Sufficient that all existence needs
51	Al-Gheyaath	The Ultimate Reliever
52	Al-Faatir	The Separator, The Divider
53	Al-Fard	The Single
54	Al-Fattaah	The Opener
55	Al-Faaliq	The Breaker
56	Al-Qadeem	The Eternally Pre-Existence Old
57	Al-Malik	The King
58	Al-Quddoos	The Chaste of all contradictions and inconsistencies
59	Al-Qawei	The Most Able and Strong
60	Al-Qareeb	The near One
61	Al-Qayyoom	The Maintainer of creation

62	Al-Qaabidh	The withholder of livelihood
63	Al-Baasit	The Expander of livelihood
64	Qadhi-ul-Haajaat	Fulfiller of Needs and Desires
65	Al-Majeed	The Most Glorious
66	Al-Mawla	The Master and Owner of souls and all creation
67	Al-Mannaan	The Gracious
68	Al-Muheet	The Ultimate Embracer of all
69	Al-Mubeen	The Manifested
70	Al-Muqeet	The Sustainer, the Reckoner of Time
71	Al-Musawwir	The Shaper of all creation
72	Al-Kareem	The Generous
73	Al-Kabeer	The Grand (the Most Great and Able)
74	Al-Kaafi	The Sufficient
75	Kaashif al-Dhor	The Remover of Calamities
76	Al-Witr	The Odd One
77	Al-Noor	The Light
78	Al-Wahhaab	The Giver
79	Al-Naasir	The Ultimate Helper
80	Al-Waasi'	The Vast, All-Encompassing, All-Embracing
81	Al-Wadood	The Loving One
82	Al-Haadi	The Guiding One
83	Al-Waafi	The Faithful and Devoted
84	Al-Wakeel	The Ultimate Trustee and Disposer of Affairs
85	Al-Waarith	The Inheritor of Everything
86	Al-Barr	The Benign, The Source of All-Goodness

87	Al-Baa'eth	The Initial Creator and Resurrector
88	Al-Tawwaab	The Granter and Accepter of repentance
89	Al-Jaleel	The Majestic over all, The Glorious
90	Al-Jawaad	The most Generous One
91	Al-Khabeer	The Expert (of the true nature of that exists)
92	Al-Khaaliq	The Creator and Inventor of all Existence
93	Khairun Naasireen	The Best of Helpers
94	Al-Dayyaan	The rewarding His believers for their deeds
95	Al-Shakoor	The Grateful (The Thankful and Appreciative)
96	Al-Adheem	The Incomparably Great
97	Al-Lateef	The Most Kind (The Gentle to His creation)
98	Al-Shaafi	The Curer
99	Al-Aaleem	The All-Knowing

HE IS BASEET[1]

God is not a substance.

Human beings are composed of many parts; eyes, ears, tongue, flesh, blood, bones... and similarly, when we look at animals we find that they too are made up of various parts and the difference between them and humans lies in their intellectual capabilities. Also, whenever we glance at other creations such as plants, rocks, water, etc., we notice that they are all made up of various substances, properties and colours. All creatures in this respect, however large or small, share this common factor.

This is not the case with God. He does not consist of parts and he is Baseet. Unlike us, He has no eyes, ears, limbs, etc. Had God possessed any of these He would have been a substance and every substance requires a second party to compose it and make it. Since nothing had existed before God, who could therefore have been He's maker?

The holy Qor'aan says:

((...NOTHING LIKE A LIKENESS OF HIM...[2])).

---

[1] Not made up of parts. (Translator).
[2] Holy Qor'aan: Soorah 42, Aayah 11.

As everything that you can think of is a substance except for God!

The Qor'aan further says:

((AND THEY HAVE NOT HONOURED ALLAAH WITH THE HONOUR THAT IS DUE TO HIM...[1])).

God has no body or limbs, nor is He a 'thing'. Unlike us, He does not consume and requires no food. He is no one's offspring and neither does He have children; as the Jews used to believe that 'Uzeir' was a child of God!! And as the Christians believed, and still do, that Christ is the son of God!

The Prophet of Islam was asked about God by a group of people. God sent him the reply in the following verse:

((SAY: HE, ALLAAH, IS ONE. ALLAAH, IS HE ON WHOM ALL DEPEND. HE BEGETS NOT, NOR IS HE BEGOTTEN. AND NONE IS LIKE HIM[2].)).

A man by the name of Mohammed Hamdaani wrote to Imaam Kaadhem[AS] the following:

((A number of your followers have a conflict of opinion on Monotheism. Some say that God is a body and others say that He is a face. The Imaam wrote in his reply:
Glorified be He Who is indefinable, and beyond description, there is nothing like Him and He is All Hearing and All Knowing[3].)).

Imaam Ja'far al Saadiq[AS] said:

---

[1] Holy Qor'aan: Soorah 39, Aayah 67.
[2] Holy Qor'aan: Soorah 112.
[3] Al-Tawheed / al-Sadooq = page 100.

((God is neither body nor face. His existence is beyond comprehension; He is not touchable and neither can He be felt by any of our senses, nor can the mind understand Him. Life cannot destroy Him and He does not fade away by time[1].))

The Imaam also told Yoonos (a narrator):

((Whoever thinks that God has a face like any other, has no religion, whoever is of the belief that God possesses a body and limbs like any other creation, is amongst the non-Believers. He further continued: The Almighty God cannot be compared to anything and nothing compares with Him. He is beyond imagination[2].))

---

[1] Behaar al-Anwaar / al-Majlesi = vol. 3, page 291.
[2] Kefaayah al-Athar / al-Khazzaaz = page 255.

HE CANNOT BE SEEN

It has been narrated that there was a man who denied the existence of God by claiming that everything which exists should be felt by at least one of the five senses; that it should either be seen, heard, smelt, tasted or touched and that with regards to God he had not seen Him, heard, smelt, tasted or felt Him.

Upon hearing these remarks, another person who was a believer in God decided to make two balls, one was made of wood and the other was made of metal and he painted them both the same colour. He then presented these two balls to the non-Believing man and asked him: "Look at these two balls, I have made one out of wood and the other of metal. Can you, by looking at them, be able to tell me which one is the metal ball and which is the wooden one?" The non-Believer observed both balls and said: "I am not able to!" The Believer then asked him: "Use your ears, perhaps you may hear something that can help you choose." The non-Believer put his ears against each ball and was none the wiser. The Believer then asked him: "Try to use your tongue and taste it." Again, the non-Believer tried and still could not distinguish. This time the Believer further asked him: "Touch them with your hands and see if perhaps this way you can tell the difference." The non-Believer felt the two balls and yet failed to distinguish. The Believer then asked him: "Well, how do you intend to tell which is metal and which is wood?" The non-Believer replied: "I shall hold both of them and the one which is heavier has to be the metal ball and the one which is lighter is the wooden ball." The Believer exclaimed: "Who is it that can certify the heavy ball is of metal?" The non-Believer replied: "My mind tells me!" The Believer immediately responded: "This simple paint had stopped you from recognising the difference and also obstructed your five senses to be able to distinguish between the two, and has made you admit to the inability of your senses but you eventually resorted to using your mind. What is therefore, preventing you to use your mind and intellect to recognise the existence of God Whose signs are apparent and evident, and to have faith in Him even though your senses may not be able to understand God?"

The non-Believer contemplated, took back his words and declared his faith in God!

Indeed, God cannot be seen as He is not a body. But the fact that we cannot see Him does not mean that He does not exist.

We cannot see the mind so how can we distinguish whether one person is intelligent and another is insane. Our judgement is based on the signs of intellect that is displayed by that person and of the signs of insanity displayed by the other.

Likewise, we do not see God but believe in His existence because we see His signs (of creation).

To be able to see God is impossible as He is not a substance and He will never be seen; not in this world and not in the Hereafter. As the holy Qor'aan says:

((VISION COMPREHENDS HIM NOT, AND HE COMPREHENDS (ALL) VISION[1].)).

((AND WHEN MOOSA (MOOSA) CAME AT OUR APPOINTED TIME AND HIS LORD SPOKE TO HIM, HE SAID: MY LORD! SHOW ME (THYSELF), SO THAT I MAY LOOK UPON THEE. HE SAID: YOU CANNOT (BEAR TO) SEE ME, BUT LOOK AT THE MOUNTAIN, IF IT REMAINS FIRM IN ITS PLACE, THEN WILL YOU SEE ME; BUT WHEN HIS LORD MANIFESTED HIS GLORY TO THE MOUNTAIN HE MADE IT CRUMBLE AND MOOSA FELL DOWN IN A SWOON[2].)).

The Almighty God refers to this great request when He tells the Prophet of Islam:

((THE FOLLOWERS OF THE BOOK ASK YOU TO BRING DOWN TO THEM A BOOK FROM HEAVEN; SO INDEED THEY DEMANDED OF MOOSA A GREATER THING THAN THAT, FOR THEY SAID: SHOW US ALLAAH MANIFESTLY; SO THE LIGHTNING OVERTOOK THEM ON ACCOUNT OF THEIR INJUSTICE[3].)).

A man who was known as Tha'lab asked Ameer al-Mo'meneen[AS]:

((Have you ever seen your God? The Imaam answered him: Alas, Tha'lab! I am not one to worship a God that I have not seen. Tha'lab then asked again: How have you seen Him, describe Him to us! The Imaam replied: The eyes do not

---

[1] Holy Qor'aan: Soorah 6, Aayah 103.
[2] Holy Qor'aan: Soorah 7, Aayah 143.
[3] Holy Qor'aan: Soorah 4, Aayah 153.

seen Him but the hearts see Him with the true faith[1].)).

Imaam Baaqir[AS] said to Abu Haashim:

((What you can see with your heart is far more accurate than what you see with your eyes, as there are times for example, when in your imagination, you can get a picture of the countries you have never visited, therefore, even the heart cannot be able to comprehend God, yet alone the eyes![2])).

There are verses in the holy Qor'aan that makes one imagine whether God is a substance or whether He could be seen:

((THE BENEFICENT GOD IS FIRM IN POWER[3].)).

(((SOME) FACES ON THAT DAY SHALL BE BRIGHT, LOOKING TO THEIR LORD[4].)).

The above verses are common expressions to describe the Power of God. For example, when it is said that "the King is on the throne" it is not meant to be taken literally, that the King is at this present moment sitting on his throne, but that it means the King is the ruler and the welfare of the state is within his power.

Another example is that if we claim that "this particular student will be a good headmaster in the near

---

[1] Behaar al-Anwaar / al-Majlesi = vol. 4, page 27.
[2] Behaar al-Anwaar / al-Majlesi = vol. 4, page 39.
[3] Holy Qor'aan: Soorah 20, Aayah 5.
[4] Holy Qor'aan: Soorah 75, Aayah 22.

future" even though he is still only a student, it is because of his potential that we look unto his future.

The meaning of the above two verses, therefore, are that: "God beholds the entire universe and on the Day of Judgement everyone will believe in His existence, as if they can see Him. Unlike when in the world, they disbelieved in Him and doubted His existence, His existence will then become clear to them."

NO TIME, NO PLACE

Time and place are the affects of substance. The space that is occupied by a substance is the actual place of that substance. The duration of substance in that place is time.

According to Einstein every substance has a length, width, height and continuation. The continuation of substance is the time of that substance. If we imagine that there exists no substance in this world, will there remain any time in the universe? Never! Because time consists of continuation.

God is exempt from 'time' and 'place'. It means that there is no place which is assigned to Him, i.e. it cannot be said that God is in the skies, on earth, in the heavens, etc.

There is also no 'time' specified for God. It cannot be said that God on Friday, in the month of Rajab, the year of one thousand and..., etc. God is not a substance. He therefore, has no duration and no place. But He is capable of seeing everything and everywhere, all from one end of the east to beyond the galaxies. Likewise, He is a witness of all times, that He can in the same instance see the past and the future. The reason that we are incapable of seeing beyond the east is because we, in the west are confined to our particular space, and that we are also incapable of seeing the past or the future because we are confined to the present time in which we live in. God however, is not engulfed in a particular surrounding and as a result sees over everything. As He is neither confined to a specific period, He also sees all seasons and periods.

If, for example, a person is born into an environment of smoke he cannot envisage another environment free from smoke as he thinks that smoke exists in all other places. But one who lives outside of that smoky environment is able to see the smoke because smoke has not covered his surroundings. Hence, whenever we imagine something we also envisage a time and place with it because we, ourselves, have been born into a time and a place. But the God that is exempt from a specific time and place can see from the beginning to the end of time and place as they do not surround Him.

It has been narrated that Imaam Ja'far Saadiq[AS] said:

((The Almighty God cannot be described by time, place speed, motion or stability as it is He Who is the Creator of time, place, motion, and stability[1].))

God is aware of all places and of all periods and holds the reins to all.

It has been narrated from Ameer al-Mo'meneen[AS] who said:

((An angel from the East came to Moosa Ibn Emraan. He asked the angel where it had come from and the angel said it came from the Almighty God. Another angel then came from the

---

[1] Al-Amaali / al-Sadooq = page 279. Behaar al-Anwaar / al-Majlesi = vol. 3, page 309.

> *West and Moosa asked again where it had come from and it said "I have come from the seventh sky and from the Almighty God." Another angel came and after Moosa asked where it had come from it said: "I am from the seventh earth below and I, too am from the Almighty God." Moosa thus claimed: "Pure is He Who is omnipresent and He is in the closest of places[1].))*

It has been narrated that Ameer al-Mo'meneen[2] once heard a person say:

> *((I swear to the One Who hides beyond the screens... To which the Imaam exclaimed: Alas! The Almighty God is too great to hide beyond anything. Pure is He Who is not confined to any space and there is nothing on earth or in the skies that is concealed to Him[3].))*

---

[1] Behaar al-Anwaar / al-Majlesi = vol. 3, page 325. Al-Ehtejaaj / al-Tabarsi = page 209.
[2] A title given to Imaam Ali, the first Caliph, by Allaah. It means: Commander of the Faithful. (Translator).
[3] Al-Ershaad / al-Mofeed = vol. 1, page 224.

HE IS NOT SUBJECT TO CHANGE

Everything that exists goes through certain changes and bears certain characteristics.

Man sleeps, moves, sits, becomes displeased or happy, eats, ages, grows helpless, puts on weight, looses weight, etc. In a lot of their habits, animals are also similar to humans. Plants also root, grow, blossom, flower, give fruit, turn colour, wither and dry up. Minerals too, harden, crumble and change colour and thus the same changes occur in other beings.

All these changes take place because of the effects of substance, therefore, one who has a heart often becomes sad and at times happy, and one with flesh and veins experiences illness and good health and one with an appetite and lustful desires eats and makes love. Whatever is of substance grows and then ages or withers and changes colour.

However, God has no body and is not of substance and as a result He does not go through turmoils; His whole essence is exempt from change.

The holy Qor'aan says in this regard:

((ALLAAH IS HE BESIDES WHOM THERE IS NO GOD, THE EVER-LIVING, THE SELF-SUBSISTING BY WHOM ALL

SUBSIST; SLUMBER DOES NOT OVERTAKE HIM NOR SLEEP...[1])).

((AND RELY ON THE EVER-LIVING WHO DIES NOT...[2])).

Imaam Moosa Ibn Ja'far[AS] said:

((The Almighty God is too grand and far greater than to be in need of limbs or to be limited to any motion or be described by height, or for the imaginations to reach Him. He descended His teachings and warnings and promises, commanding without the use lip or tongue[3].)).

---

[1] Holy Qor'aan: Soorah 2, Aayah 155.
[2] Holy Qor'aan: Soorah 25, Aayah 58.
[3] Al-Tawheed / al-Sadooq = page 75.

PART II:
JUSTICE

GOD IS JUST

There are times when we come across incidents in which a person who is to pass a judgement rules unjustly. If we were to find out the reasons for this injustice we will notice that he has done so for one of the following reasons:

1- He was ignorant of the truth and thus acted unjustly
2- He aimed to gain a benefit, i.e. he had been bribed
3- To protect himself, for example, he could endanger his life if he were to act upon the truth
4- With his injustice he aimed to defend his own friends or family
5- He is a corrupt and dishonest person who defies the truth

These are the reasons for the miscarriages of justice. We will, at a later stage, look at the motives for such an injustice.

It could therefore be due to one of the above reasons that motivates a person who is sitting in judgement to give precedence to one who is vile and wicked rather than to one who is more worthy and deserves to be justly treated. Also, a person who shows more respect to people who are indecent but abuses those who are righteous and have higher merits is also doing so because of the above reasons.

There is a sixth reason as to why one would act unjustly and that is because of a weakness. It could be that this person himself had been unfairly treated and as he could not stand up for his own rights and defend himself, he instead inflicts his enmity on others and abuses their rights. These are the motives for cruelty and injustice.

Can any of these motives be found in God that would drive Him to cruelty? Never! God is not ignorant and does not need to either win or lose and is not biased towards anyone, on the contrary, everyone is His creation and there is no family or friend in between them; corruption does not exist in His pure nature and He has no weaknesses, therefore, why should He be unjust?

The Divine Justice is widely spread and extensive and unlike what we imagine it to be, is not restricted:

- With His Creation God is Just and does not set rules that are unfair.
- God is just in His Divine Decree and Judgement. He does not therefore enrich, impoverish, endear, give life, take life and inflict pain upon anyone without justification. He does not give or take from anyone….unless it is justified.
- In Creation He is Just, therefore, the dazzling sun, the illuminating moon, the sparkling stars, the roaring seas, the vast earth, plants, animals and humans have not been created irrationally.
- In His Commandments and Prohibitions He is Just. He sets out obligatory rules and sets rewards

for the recommended ones (non-obligatory), He forbids unlawful acts and is displeased with those acts that are undesirable and allows for the use of all things lawful ... according to justice.

The lack of foresight in man's intellect at times disables him to understand the way in which Divine Justice is carried out. In such cases, the fault lies with us and not in the Divine Justice. As is the case with children, for example, they are not aware of the benefits of a medication and resist taking it and may develop a dislike for the doctor. The problem here is in the child's ignorance and not the medication of the doctor.

We, too, cannot understand many of the universal affairs and its purpose; does it mean that we should therefore deny its existence? Of course not. The fact that we are able to comprehend some of its affairs and justices should be sufficient for us to have belief in the Divine justice. If we cannot understand the medication prescribed by a doctor, even though we know him to be a reputable doctor, it is not right to be displeased with him just because we dislike taking his medication.

With regards to the Divine Justice the holy Qor'aan states:

((THIS IS FOR WHAT YOUR OWN HANDS HAVE SENT BEFORE AND BECAUSE ALLAAH IS NOT IN THE LEAST UNJUST TO THE SERVANTS[1].))

((SURELY ALLAAH DOES NOT DO INJUSTICE TO THE WEIGHT OF A SMALL ANT, AND IF IT IS A GOOD DEED HE

---

[1] Holy Qor'aan: Soorah 3, Aayah 182.

MULTIPLIES IT AND GIVES FROM HIMSELF A GREAT REWARD[1].)).

((...AND THEY SHALL NOT BE WRONGED...[2])).

((...SO IT WAS NOT ALLAAH WHO SHOULD DO THEM INJUSTICE, BUT THEY WERE UNJUST TO THEMSELVES[3].)).

((...ALLAAH WAS NOT UNJUST TO THEM, BUT THEY WERE UNJUST TO THEMSELVES.
SO THE EVIL (CONSEQUENCES) OF WHAT THEY DID SHALL AFFLICT THEM AND THAT WHICH THEY MOCKED SHALL ENCOMPASS THEM[4].)).

((...ALLAAH DOES NOT DESIRE INJUSTICE FOR (HIS) SERVANTS[5].)).

((THIS DAY EVERY SOUL SHALL BE REWARDED FOR WHAT IT HAS EARNED; NO INJUSTICE (SHALL BE DONE) THIS DAY; SURELY ALLAAH IS QUICK IN RECKONING[6].)).

Ameer al-Mo'meneen[(AS)][7] was asked about the Tawheed and the Justice of Allaah to which he replied:

((Tawheed is that you do not imagine Him; and Justice is that you do not accuse Him[8].)).

---

[1] Holy Qor'aan: Soorah 4, Aayah 40.
[2] Holy Qor'aan: Soorah 4, Aayah 49.
[3] Holy Qor'aan: Soorah 9, Aayah 70.
[4] Holy Qor'aan: Soorah 16, Aayaat 33-34.
[5] Holy Qor'aan: Soorah 40, Aayah 31.
[6] Holy Qor'aan: Soorah 40, Aayah 17.
[7] *Alayhes Salaam* = Peace be upon him.
[8] Behaar al-Anwaar / al-Majlesi = vol. 5, page 52.

Imaam Saadiq[AS] was asked about Justice to which he replied:

((Justice is that you do not attribute to your creator that which He admonishes you for[1].)).

He also said:

((...And He does not command of you something unless He knows that you are capable of fulfilling because the nature of God is exempt from injustice, uselessness and setting tasks that He knows man is incapable of achieving[2].)).

In another narration it comes that:

((The skies stand upon justice.)).

---

[1] Al-Tawheed / al-Sadooq = page 96.
[2] Al-Ehtejaaj / al-Tabarsi = page 341.

QADHAA AND QADAR[1]

Qadhaa and Qadar fall into three categories:

1- In the Creation of the Universe: God passed a decree for the creation of the heavens and the earth and predestined the sustenance of His creation. In this respect all the creation that exist within the universe are as a result of Qadhaa and Qadar and this universe does not, to any extent, work against His will; this fact is very clear and those who believe in God also have belief in this.

2- Qadhaa and Qadar in the Law: God has implemented His laws of religion; He has ordered people to certain commands and acts and

---

[1] 'Qadhaa' is an order and command from God. There are rules that God sets and to which He orders us to and we have to implement and put into practice. 'Qadar' is the measure that God sets and again, which we have to apply. (Examples of 'Qadhaa and Qadar' and the different categories they fall into are explained in the text)

Since it is only God Who can set such orders and measures 'Qadhaa and Qadar' are therefore from God only (hence, wherever the words 'Qadhaa and Qadar appear in any text it is meant as the Divine Qadhaa and Qadar). (Translator).

prohibited them of others. He has set some obligatory acts, some that are non-obligatory and some that are undesirable. Therefore, performing the obligatory prayers and the prohibition of alcohol consumption are also of Qadhaa and Qadar.

3- Qadhaa and Qadar in People's Deeds: The decree of God with regard to the actions of His people falls into the following thoughts:

i) Encouraging of good deeds and discouraging of bad ones.
ii) Knowledge in whatever people do, i.e. their good and their bad deeds, their obedience and disobedience. This is also very clear, as we had mentioned before, God has the knowledge of all things and that there is nothing on earth or the heavens which is concealed to Him.
iii) To think that God forces people in their deeds and that no one has the power over their own actions! This thought is wrong and its invalidity is as clear as daylight because it is self-evident that we perform our deeds by our own will and desires; if we wish to, we can do a good or a bad deed.

The holy Qor'aan refers to the initial part of Qadhaa and Qadar, the creation of the world, in the following:

((THEN HE DIRECTED HIMSELF TO THE HEAVEN AND IT IS A VAPOUR, SO HE SAID TO IT AND TO THE EARTH: COME BOTH, WILLINGLY OR UNWILLINGLY. THEY BOTH SAID: WE COME WILLINGLY.

SO HE ORDAINED THEM SEVEN HEAVENS IN TWO PERIODS, AND REVEALED IN EVERY HEAVEN ITS AFFAIR; AND WE ADORNED THE LOWER HEAVEN WITH BRILLIANT STARS AND (MADE IT) TO GUARD; THAT IS THE DECREE OF THE MIGHTY, THE KNOWING[1].))

And with regard to the second part of Qadhaa and Qadar, the laws, it says:

((AND YOUR LORD HAS COMMANDED THAT YOU SHALL NOT SERVE (ANY) BUT HIM, AND GOODNESS TO YOUR PARENTS[2].))

And of the third part, people's deeds, it further says:

((AND KEEP UP PRAYER AND PAY THE POOR-RATE[3]/[4].))

((SURELY ALLAAH ENJOINS THE DOING OF JUSTICE AND THE DOING OF GOOD (TO OTHERS) AND THE GIVING TO THE KINDRED, AND HE FORBIDS INDECENCY AND EVIL AND REBELLION; HE ADMONISHES YOU THAT YOU MAY BE MINDFUL[5].))

((...DO NOT SPY NOR LET SOME OF YOU BACKBITE OTHERS[6].))

It is such verses that order mankind to good deeds and bans them from evil ones.

---

[1] Holy Qor'aan: Soorah 41, Aayaat 11-12.
[2] Holy Qor'aan: Soorah 17, Aayah 23.
[3] Alms
[4] Holy Qor'aan: Soorah 2, Aayah 110.
[5] Holy Qor'aan: Soorah 16, Aayah 90.
[6] Holy Qor'aan: Soorah 49, Aayah 12.

((ALLAAH IS HE WHO CREATED SEVEN HEAVENS, AND OF THE EARTH THE LIKE OF THEM; THE DECREE CONTINUES TO DESCEND AMONG THEM, THAT YOU MAY KNOW THAT ALLAAH HAS POWER OVER ALL THINGS AND THAT ALLAAH INDEED ENCOMPASSES ALL THINGS IN (HIS) KNOWLEDGE[1].)).

And other verses which emphasis upon the knowledge that God possesses and which we have already referred to, that He is aware of all things:

*((THOSE WHO ARE POLYTHEISTS WILL SAY: IF ALLAAH HAD PLEASED WE WOULD NOT HAVE ASSOCIATED (AUGHT WITH HIM) NOR OUR FATHERS, NOR WOULD WE HAVE FORBIDDEN (TO OURSELVES) ANYTHING; EVEN SO DID THOSE BEFORE THEM REJECT UNTIL THEY TASTED OUR PUNISHMENT. SAY: HAVE YOU ANY KNOWLEDGE WITH YOU SO YOU SHOULD BRING IT FORTH TO US? YOU ONLY FOLLOW A CONJECTURE AND YOU ONLY TELL US LIES.
SAY: THEN ALLAAH'S IS THE CONCLUSIVE ARGUMENT; SO IF HE PLEASES, HE WOULD CERTAINLY GUIDE YOU ALL[2].))*.

The creation is therefore, the work of God and He has no partner in this. Only He is worthy of setting the rules and no one has the right to interfere.

With regard to the actions of individuals, God commands good deeds from them and bans them from indecent acts. He is fully aware of everyone's conduct. Each individual has the will and control over their own actions in which they have the ability to either carry out or abandon.

---

[1] Holy Qor'aan: Soorah 65, Aayah 12.
[2] Holy Qor'aan: Soorah 6, Aayaat 148-149.

FORCE AND CHOICE

An object has no control over itself, if it is thrown up gravity pulls it back down to itself. Plants have no control either as heat, light, water and soil are responsible for its growth. Water, too, has no control; if it is obstructed it cannot flow otherwise it runs through. The same applies to the sun, the moon, the stars, clouds and the wind; they all circulate upon specific and accurate rules by the will and the ability of God.

It is a human being that falls into two parts:

1- Its Formation: In this part it is the same as other creations; that its circulation of blood, its heart beat, the movement of lungs, the liver or the stomach have no control of themselves and are all totally dependent upon that which God has assigned for the body.
2- Its Will: A human is free in this respect and has control over his actions; he can sleep, eat, drink and walk whenever he wishes to. His actions, thoughts, intellect, ignorance, his sense of decency, his evilness are all of his own will and within his control.

Whoever thinks that a human is forced into his actions just like a stone is thrown without its control or a plant which grows without its will, is denying a fact that is very clear and evident. If this trait of thought is correct and a being has no control over itself then it could be argued that the laws, the judicial system and the worldly affairs are all useless. No one can make such a claim unless they are beyond humanity. Since animals have control over their own actions, can it be claimed otherwise for humans who are even far more superior than animals?!

According to the holy Qor'aan:

((AND SAY: THE TRUTH IS FROM YOUR LORD, SO LET HIM WHO PLEASES BELIEVE, AND LET HIM WHO PLEASES DISBELIEVE[1].)).

((SAY: O PEOPLE! INDEED THERE HAS COME TO YOU THE TRUTH FROM YOUR LORD, THEREFORE WHOEVER GOES ARIGHT, HE GOES ARIGHT ONLY FOR THE GOOD OF HIS OWN SOUL, AND WHOEVER GOES ASTRAY, HE GOES ASTRAY ONLY TO THE DETRIMENT OF IT, AND I AM NOT A CUSTODIAN OVER YOU[2].)).

((SURELY WE HAVE SHOWN HIM THE WAY: HE MAY BE THANKFUL OR UNTHANKFUL[3].)).

((AND WE HAVE POINTED OUT TO HIM THE TWO CONSPICUOUS WAYS[4].)).

---

[1] Holy Qor'aan: Soorah 18, Aayah 29.
[2] Holy Qor'aan: Soorah 10, Aayah 108.
[3] Holy Qor'aan: Soorah 76, Aayah 3.
[4] Holy Qor'aan: Soorah 90, Aayah 10.

((AND SAY: WORK; SO ALLAAH WILL SEE YOUR WORK AND (SO WILL) HIS APOSTLE AND THE BELIEVERS; AND YOU SHALL BE BROUGHT BACK TO THE KNOWER OF THE UNSEEN AND THE SEEN, THEN HE WILL INFORM YOU OF WHAT YOU DID[1].))

It has been narrated from Imaam Hosayn(AS) who said:

((A man from Iraq once approached Imaam Ali(AS) and said: Tell us whether our war with the Syrians is the Divine Qadhaa and Qadar?
Imaam Ali(AS): Indeed! I swear to the Almighty God that you do not climb a hill or walk the desert unless it is of Qadhaa and Qadar.
The man then said: In that case whatever hardship that befalls us we can put it down to God.
Imaam Ali(AS): Alas ye old man! Perhaps you think that God's Qadhaa and Qadar in people's fate is a definite and an unviolated one? If this be the case then there would be no order or ban and a promise or a threat will hold no significance, there would be no punishment for the wrongdoers and the good would go unrewarded whilst they be reprimanded for being righteous and the bad would be rewarded for their evil deeds. No! What you have claimed is the talk of the idol-worshippers and the enemies of God and the fatalists.
God orders mankind to righteousness of their own will and accord and fearfully prohibits them from evil deeds. The fact that they disobey His commands is not because they are helpless and those who obey Him are not doing so under

---

[1] Holy Qor'aan: Soorah 9, Aayah 105.

duress; and the heavens, the earth and all that is in between them have not been created aimlessly. "...THAT IS THE OPINION OF THOSE WHO DISBELIEVE; THEN WOE TO THOSE WHO DISBELIEVE ON ACCOUNT OF THE FIRE[1]".
The old man then stood up saying: You are indeed the leader of whom obedience will grant me God's forgiveness. Those parts of religion that we were ignorant of, you have made clear, may God grant you rewards for this good deed...[2])).

The rest of this incident is told in another narration:

((The old man then asked Imaam Ali[AS]: Then what is the meaning of Qadhaa and Qadar which draws us to all directions, whilst we do not walk the desert or climb any hills unless it is through Qadhaa and Qadar?
Imaam Ali[AS] replied: Order and command is from God. He then recited the following Qor'aan verse:
"AND YOUR LORD HAS COMMANDED THAT YOU SHALL NOT SERVE (ANY) BUT HIM, AND GOODNESS TO YOUR PARENTS[3]"[4].)).

Many people think that because God has set an order and that the Divine fate is definite they no longer are required to strive and work! But note how the holy Qor'aan responds to such idleness:

---

[1] Holy Qor'aan: Soorah 39, Aayah 27.
[2] Kashf al-Ghommah / al-Erbelli = vol. 2, page 288.
[3] Holy Qor'aan: Soorah 17, Aayah 23.
[4] Al-Tawheed / al-Sadooq = page 382.

((AND THAT MAN SHALL HAVE NOTHING BUT WHAT HE STRIVES FOR.
AND THAT HIS STRIVING SHALL SOON BE SEEN[1].))

((...EVERY MAN IS RESPONSIBLE FOR WHAT HE SHALL HAVE WROUGHT[2].))

((AND SAY: WORK; SO ALLAAH WILL SEE YOUR WORK AND (SO WILL) HIS APOSTLE AND THE BELIEVERS...[3]))

All the Prophets, who knew more about Qadhaa and Qadar than the rest of the people, worked throughout their lives and strived hard with determination. Likewise, the holy A'emmah[4], leaders and the guardians were all actively working. Therefore, to rely upon Qadhaa and Qadar[5] is wrong and is taken advantage of. Those who aim to disassociate themselves from their social responsibilities and deeds are using it as an excuse.

---

[1] Holy Qor'aan: Soorah 53, Aayaat 39-40.
[2] Holy Qor'aan: Soorah 52, Aayah 21.
[3] Holy Qor'aan: Soorah 9, Aayah 105.
[4] Plural of Imaam. (Translator).
[5] The belief in Qadhaa and Qadar is a must but to rely upon it whereby one would refuse to put in the personal effort in the opinion that since Qadhaa and Qadar is from God one no longer has to bear any responsibility over their actions is wrong. (Translator).

PART III:
PROPHETHOOD

THE HOLY PROPHET

Have you ever paid any attention to the corrupted life of today which is run by the governments throughout the world? Have you noticed that the bloodied wars and the colonisations happen through the laws of civilisation!

Have you ever wondered how much a person suffers at the hands of their family, society and by the status of their country? And that how they have been deprived of their peace and tranquillity? Have you ever realised that the so called 'free' man has his hands tied, his feet shackled and his neck strapped, his lips, eyes and ears are all under scrutiny and that the harder he tries the less he gains and that all these conditions and restrictions stem from people's ignorance who fall into the trap of colonisation and independence set up by those who aim to make a personal profit.

Man indeed goes through difficult periods. From the moment he is conceived into a being he becomes trapped into the darkness of the womb, following which he is restrained to the cradle. The moment he reaches puberty and thinks that he has escaped the last of the entrapments he finds that the oppressive influence of ignorance and greed, the evil diseases and corruption are surrounding him from all sides. Man therefore, in this world goes through one imprisonment to another until he eventually is imprisoned!

God has created the universe on a just and equal balance; everything has an aptitude and for every movement and motion He has set specific rules. If one part of the universe was to violate the universal rule and order, not only does the universe become corrupted but it also causes the corruption of all creation within the universe. A human being is one of the vital parts of this universe for whom God has set firm rules and order. No one but God, or one to whom God has assigned the reins of affairs and taught him the ropes can comprehend any of this.

> *((AND WITH HIM ARE THE KEYS OF THE UNSEEN TREASURES – NONE KNOWS THEM BUT HE[1].))*.

The Prophets are the only ones who know of the Divine rules and order and it is they who become aware of the virtues and weaknesses, and of the decline and the progression of the society. But other people have not understood the precise rules and if they were to take it upon themselves to create set of laws and regulations they will create nothing but corruption and demoralisation therefore, only chaos, anarchy, indecency and oppression would rule over people, the flame of wars would erupt and the bonds of societies would disperse.

Let us imagine a human member of a society as a tool and the screws of a machinery: when the tools and pieces of a machinery fall apart no one but a skilled engineer who has the expertise in this field is able to put it together and make it as good as new. But if an inexperienced person was to put this machinery together, regardless of his strength or wealth at his disposal, he will only disable and destroy it. Say, for

---

[1] Holy Qor'aan: Soorah 6, Aayah 59.

instance, he was able to put the pieces together somehow imperfectly, he still would not succeed because the tools that were not used according to their specific functions would not work properly or that the machinery would not function as it should do.

Likewise, the same should apply to human beings who are the tools of the creation. Each individual should be placed within their specific suitable environment and should be given a sense of direction that can benefit the society. A precise and logical program needs to be mapped out but at the initial stages it is necessary to form and mould the personalities of each individual so that they could be good enough as members of a virtuous society. The next stage would be to set an order for the families so that each member of that family is able to raise another decent family from which an honest and a respectable government could be formed. A government that is capable of setting up adequate and progressive laws which can also take care of the religious welfare of the public and protect the society under its wings so that everything is based upon the foundation of justice and morality.

One who can set up such precise order for mankind cannot be any other but God; the same Creator that knows only too well the good, the bad, the ugly, the beautiful and knows exactly of man's needs and future. One who is capable of implementing this Divine programme cannot be any other than a Prophet who receives Divine Revelations[1], or God's most trusted deputies.

Looking back to the history of mankind, those nations that followed the guidance of the Prophets and the path that was enlightened by the Divine Revelations rarely suffered misery and corruption. In fact, corruption and deprivation

---

[1] The Islamic commands and the Holy Book were revealed to the Prophet from God through the Angel Gabriel. (Translator).

were almost wiped out and that particular nation lived a life of peace and prosperity. Vice versa, those nations who had defied their prophets and failed to follow their commands and guidance lived in darkness and led a life of loss and adversity.

For this reasoning one example should be sufficient; the Moslems of the early Islamic era who had followed the Islamic teachings for half a century had made such an advanced progress that they ruled over the world and their affairs were well set up and organised. Their population was condensed and they were powerful. Their grand status was apparent to all. It was as a result of their obedience to the Islamic principles that they could free themselves from superstitions. But whilst the Moslems were advancing ahead of the rest of the world, the Europeans were dwelling in cruelty and disarray, other dictators and tyrannical powers ruled over them, they were being slaughtered by other blood thirsty nations and were suppressed by their kings and the courtiers... until a century ago, whether knowingly or otherwise, they adopted some of the Islamic teachings and began to reconstruct themselves. They gained some rule and order and with some of the Islamic training that were used, they began to experience peace and security.

I am not alone in making such a claim but George Jardaq, who was a Christian and had never been a Moslem, in his book titled "Imaam Ali - The Voice of Human Justice"[1] writes: "Ali[(AS)2] who had himself confessed to being one of the servants of the Prophet Mohammed was more advanced in human rights welfare twelve centuries ago than the current French intellectuals, because the laws of Ali[(AS)] with regard

---

[1] Imaam Ali[(AS)] was the son-in-law of the holy Prophet, his cousin and after the Prophet's martyrdom, the first Imaam (leader). (Translator).

[2] *Alayhes Salaam* = Peace be upon him.

to human rights and justice stand upon the precious foundation of integrity and dedication."

We have witnessed for ourselves how France, who claims to be the legislator of human rights laws, has kicked aside such laws and rights and with great impudence massacred thousands of Algerians and drowned the cries of those seeking their rights and freedom with bullets.

Indeed, only the Prophets were capable of establishing justified laws and it was only they who could, through the Divine Revelation, implement such meticulous and organised order for mankind.

If we focus upon the rules that govern the people today, and thus compare them to the Islamic rules, we will find that a great difference lies between the two and will notice how far apart they are from each other. Only then do we realise that most of the cold and bloody wars that erupt everywhere and all the time are as a result of people deviating from the Prophetic guidance and that people have been selfish and self-ruled whilst establishing their own regulations. We would also realise that if in place of man-made laws, religious order and Prophetic teachings were to rule, everyone would have dwelled under the canopy of justice and rectitude, peace, tranquillity and brotherhood.

All the calamities that are inflicted upon man; the pressures, the slavery, the humiliations, etc. stem from corruption and a cruel system that has deviated from the right path of God and His Prophets.

Man will continue to experience the intolerable misfortunes of ignorance, poverty, illness, wars, disorder and numerous other problems until he begins to realise his worth and understand what is right for him. He will then rush towards making his happiness and befriend himself with the Divine laws and thus cast away the oppressive laws of dictators. This day will soon arrive and we shall wait for such a day by counting its every minute.

RELIGION AND MAN-MADE LAWS

There are two major differences between man-made laws and the divine laws:

1- The first difference: It is correct that the man-made laws, in the best of conditions, are set up by a group of intellectuals and wise individuals but we ask the following questions:

- Have these intelligent policy makers taken into account the rights and the opinions of the people of the west and the east side of the universe or are their policies based upon the people living around their own environment? Most certainly they act upon their own perceptions; and
- Do they take into consideration all the conditions that apply to the present time and the future, or do they simply base their policies upon the circumstances of that particular period and environment?
- Are these group of policy makers immune from errors and corruption? Or are their level

of intellect and knowledge extensive, unlimited and infinite?

These are the type of questions that arise with regard to the making of the laws of human rights. The answers to these are very clear:

The thinking of this group is derived from specific environment, circumstances, time and people, and their intellectual minds are not immune from errors. At times they fail and at other times they can correctly distinguish the truth.

In such a case how is it possible to fully trust their judgement and implement their laws onto people? Even though many of these intellectuals and human rights legislators are capable of making the correct judgement, they may be influenced by the prejudice and greed that surrounds them.

One important factor here is that even if the legislators themselves are not capable of corruption they are, nevertheless, under the scrutiny and the influence of their own government and as we can see for ourselves the dictatorial governments set up their own parliaments and constitutions and from behind the closed doors, push through their own inhumane rules and regulations and thus force their immoral desires, disguised as 'laws', upon other powerless nations.

This method of legislation is completely against the religion because the legislator of religion is God Who does not aim His laws at just one particular group or nation, or for a specific time zone and environment; the God that neither desires nor temptations can corrupt Him, the God Who is not ignorant of any issues or situation. As well as all these, God is kinder to His creatures than anyone else can ever be and it is on such basis that His commands are virtuous and beneficial. His laws are just and fair and His plans are solid and firm.

> ((...AND WHAT IS THERE AFTER THE TRUTH BUT ERROR[1].)).

2- The second difference: The difference between the man-made laws and the divine laws is that the man-made laws take into consideration the physical needs only and have been drawn up to deal with the cases of buying and selling, marriage and divorce, renting and letting, teachings and professions, agriculture, stealing, and combat against drugs and other physical needs.

However, the divine laws take into consideration both, the physical and the spiritual needs. Just as the divine laws take care of buying and selling, they also care about cheating and honesty within dealing; such laws urge people involved in business transactions to take into consideration the welfare of the other party. Whilst the divine laws urge people to education, they also require of them sincerity and good heartedness. Whilst the laws propagate agriculture, they also propagate righteousness and belief in God.

Most importantly, for the purification of the heart the divine laws forbid acts of jealousy, selfishness, self-righteousness, self-publicity and greed for power whilst on the other hand, these laws beautify the hearts of their followers by strengthening feelings of affection and sentiments, encouraging good deeds, pleasantness and sincerity and disliking for them evil deeds.

The divine laws forbid the tongue to lie, gossip, backbite and slander. They forbid the stomach to consume

---

[1] Holy Qor'aan: Soorah 10, Aayah 32.

from unlawful earnings and forbid the sensual senses and desires to indulge in acts of adultery and homosexuality. Likewise, for the purification of the hands, feet, ears, eyes and every part of the body and senses such laws have assigned specific tasks.

That is why the man-made laws seem to be dreary and soulless, as opposed to religious laws which are pleasant, fulfilling; they grow and move ahead, blossom and bear their fruits…

To look back to the history of mankind one will see that those nations that were governed by religious laws dwelled in security, peace, equality and justice and lived within the sentiments of brotherhood and friendship. But instead, those nations that rejected religion and refused to be governed by its laws and ethics were marred by extensive cruelty, injustice, corruption and disorder and their societies were totally drowned in immorality.

THE PROPHETS AND THE PROPHET OF ISLAM

The divine laws and the religions that were introduced by God did not differ from one another. In order to accommodate the different times and the progression of the societies their forms and methods varied slightly but these differences were not substantial.

The Prophets were all brothers even though their mothers and fathers were different. Adam, Nooh, Ebraaheem, Moosa, Easa[1], Mohammad were all sent by the One God, their call was one, their aim was one and their path and methods were one. All the Prophets ordered people to righteousness and forbade them from bad deeds. All of them guided people towards the truth and established justice. The source of their knowledge was revelations: the Divine messages of God; and the foundation of their task was based on the awakening of man's conscious and inviting him to justice and truth.

The first Prophet acknowledged the last Prophet and the last Prophet acknowledged the first, and the other

---

[1] Also Jesus.

Prophets approved all the previous ones hence they propagated and prepared people for the future Prophets.

It is on such basis that we do not see a major difference in the mission of the Prophets, although there are people who corrupt and alter the divine laws in order to suit their own wishes and desires and there are politicians too who, for their own political gain and policies, alter the Holy Books just as the Bible and the Turat[1] were distorted and interfered with.

This is one of the distinctions that separate the divine laws from the man-made laws, because no matter what any intellectual or philosopher, parliament, legislator, or a despotic government produces, in fortification and reliability they can never match the divine laws. The divine laws are based upon a firm and solid foundation with pillars that are indestructible.

Each Prophet acknowledged the other and together, they invited people to follow the teachings of the forthcoming Prophets. The holy Qor'aan refers to this in its following verses:

((NAY! WERE YOU WITNESSES WHEN DEATH VISITED YA'QOOB, WHEN HE SAID TO HIS SONS: WHAT WILL YOU SERVE AFTER ME? THEY SAID: WE WILL SERVE YOUR GOD AND THE GOD OF YOUR FATHERS, EBRAAHEEM AND ISMAIL AND ESHAAQ, ONE GOD ONLY, AND TO HIM DO WE SUBMIT[2].))

((SAY: WE BELIEVE IN ALLAAH AND (IN) THAT WHICH HAD BEEN REVEALED TO US, AND (IN) THAT WHICH WAS REVEALED TO EBRAAHEEM, AND ISMAIL AND ESHAAQ AND YA'QOOB AND THE TRIBES, AND (IN) THAT WHICH WAS GIVEN TO MOOSA AND EASA, AND (IN) THAT

---

[1] The Holy Book descended upon the Prophet Moosa. (Translator).
[2] Holy Qor'aan: Soorah 2, Aayah 133.

WHICH WAS GIVEN TO THE PROPHETS FROM THEIR LORD, WE DO NOT MAKE ANY DISTINCTION BETWEEN ANY OF THEM, AND TO HIM DO WE SUBMIT.

IF THEN THEY BELIEVE AS YOU BELIEVE IN HIM, THEY ARE INDEED ON THE RIGHT COURSE, AND IF THEY TURN BACK, THEN THEY ARE ONLY IN GREAT OPPOSITION, SO ALLAAH WILL SUFFICE YOU AGAINST THEM, AND HE IS THE HEARING, THE KNOWING[1].)).

---

[1] Holy Qor'aan: Soorah 2, Aayah 136-137.

WHAT IS RELIGION?

Religion is based upon the following four pillars:

1- Belief
2- Virtue (or morals)
3- Worship
4- Other deeds...

These four are rational fundamentals that are naturally in tune with man's intellect. All the religions, however different they may appear to be (due to the change of times and the circumstances of the society), still share the same role of calling for these four main principles.

We will briefly discuss these four common principles and will further continue on our topic of Prophethood.

1: BELIEF

In Islam, belief falls back onto three main foundations:

First: Belief in the God - the Creator of all things, who is Alive, Everlasting, Able, Wise, Knowledgeable and a Provider. He has no spouse or children and neither does He have an associate to share His sovereignty with. He is a Judge that carries no injustice or cruelty. He is immensely kind, cares for His creatures and is the King of the heavens and the earth.

And belief in the Divine Angels who are the supreme creatures of God and who never disobey God's command. The holy Qor'aan says:

> *((SAY: O FOLLOWERS OF THE BOOK! COME TO AN EQUITABLE PROPOSITION BETWEEN US AND YOU THAT WE SHALL NOT SERVE ANY BUT ALLAAH AND (THAT) WE SHALL NOT ASSOCIATE OUGHT WITH HIM, AND (THAT) SOME OF US SHALL NOT TAKE OTHERS FOR LORDS BESIDES ALLAAH; BUT IF THEY TURN BACK, THEN SAY: BEAR WITNESS THAT WE ARE MUSLIMS[1].))*.

Will the mind ever believe that: Easa[2] or any other of the prophets of God would invite people to polytheism, or to associate with God traits such as cruelty, ignorance, and weakness…? Indeed not; never!

Second: Belief in the Prophets of God and in their successors; those who were before them and those who succeed them. This means that God has sent His deputies and Messengers in order to guide mankind to the truth and the right path, and to save them from corruption, greed, destruction, misery, etc. As we had discussed before, the first prophet acknowledged the last prophet and the last prophet approved the first and the ones who were sent in between always acknowledged the past prophets and announced the coming of the future ones. Likewise, their successors also acknowledged each other, as we shall see when we come to discuss this further under the topic of leadership.

---

[1] Holy Qor'aan: Soorah 3, Aayah 64.
[2] Also Jesus.

The situation of the prophets and their successors in this regard, is exactly the same as that of the governors who are elected by their governments and are sent one after another to govern different provinces. The first governor knows that another governor will succeed him, and the last governor knows that there was one before him. They all approve the same principles upon which their work is based.

In the holy Qor'aan God refers to the prophethood of Easa:

((...VERIFYING WHAT WAS BEFORE IT OF TAWRAAT[1]...[2])).

((AND WHEN EASA SON OF MARYAM SAID: O CHILDREN OF ISRAEL! SURELY I AM THE APOSTLE OF ALLAAH TO YOU, VERIFYING THAT WHICH IS BEFORE ME OF THE TAWRAAT AND GIVING THE GOOD NEWS OF AN APOSTLE WHO WILL COME AFTER ME, HIS NAME BEING AHMAD[3]...[4])).

With regards to the prophethood of Ebraaheem and of when he requested God to send the prophet Mohammed, the holy Qor'aan quotes him saying:

((OUR LORD! AND RAISE UP IN THEM AN APOSTLE FROM AMONG THEM WHO SHALL RECITE TO THEM THY COMMUNICATIONS AND TEACH THEM THE BOOK AND THE WISDOM, AND PURIFY THEM; SURELY THOU ART THE MIGHTY, THE WISE[5].)).

---

[1] The Holy Book that was descended upon the Prophet Moosa. (Translator).
[2] Holy Qor'aan: Soorah 5, Aayah 46.
[3] Another name of the Prophet Mohammed. (Translator).
[4] Holy Qor'aan: Soorah 61, Aayah 6.
[5] Holy Qor'aan: Soorah 2, Aayah 129.

And With regards to the acknowledgement of our prophet Mohammed by the previous prophets, it says:

((SAY: WE BELIEVE IN ALLAAH AND (IN) THAT WHICH HAD BEEN REVEALED TO US, AND (IN) THAT WHICH WAS REVEALED TO EBRAAHEEM AND ISMAIL AND ESHAAQ AND YA'QOOB[1] AND THE TRIBES, AND (IN) THAT WHICH WAS GIVEN TO MOOSA[2] AND EASA, AND (IN) THAT WHICH WAS GIVEN TO THE PROPHETS FROM THEIR LORD, WE DO NOT MAKE ANY DISTINCTION BETWEEN ANY OF THEM, AND TO HIM DO WE SUBMIT[3].))

((AND WHO FORSAKES THE RELIGION OF EBRAAHEEM BUT HE WHO MAKES HIMSELF A FOOL, AND MOST CERTAINLY WE CHOSE HIM (EBRAAHEEM) IN THIS WORLD, AND IN THE HEREAFTER HE IS MOST SURELY AMONG THE RIGHTEOUS[4].))

((THE APOSTLE (MOHAMMED) BELIEVES IN WHAT HAS BEEN REVEALED TO HIM FROM HIS LORD, AND (SO DO) THE BELIEVERS; THEY ALL BELIEVE IN ALLAAH AND HIS ANGELS AND HIS BOOKS AND HIS APOSTLES; WE MAKE NO DIFFERENCE BETWEEN ANY OF HIS APOSTLES...[5]))

All the divine prophets had the same objectives and God knows every one of them, from the first to the last, therefore why should He not have informed each one of them so that they could pass on to their followers the news of the coming prophet? All the prophets aimed towards the same truth and are were the representatives of the One God;

---

[1] They are all prophets. (Translator).
[2] Also Moses.
[3] Holy Qor'aan: Soorah 2, Aayah 136.
[4] Holy Qor'aan: Soorah 2, Aayah 130.
[5] Holy Qor'aan: Soorah 2, Aayah 285.

therefore, why should they not have sought the allegiance of their followers for the next prophet? On this basis, all the nations are the same, as they are the nation of the One God and the subject of One King. As the holy Qor'aan says:

> *((SURELY THIS ISLAM IS YOUR RELIGION, ONE RELIGION (ONLY), AND I AM YOUR LORD, THEREFORE SERVE ME*[1]*.))*.

To the disappointment of those Christians who, for their own personal gain, altered and distorted the holy Books of Tawraat and the Bible and omitted the passages that were about the coming of the Prophet of Islam, there can still be found certain passages amongst the pages of these holy Books that inform people of a prophet who is to follow after Easa.

Third: Belief in the Day of Judgement and the resurrection of the dead after their bodies have turned into dust and demolished. God resurrects all so that the righteous ones are rewarded for their good deeds and the bad are punished. The Day of Resurrection is the day when God gathers all humans in a vast desert by the name of 'Mahshar' and judgement takes place. Every individual's book of deeds is opened up in front of them and when they look on they see that everything that they had done, however big or small, has been recorded in this book! It is here that those who pursued falsehood perish and those who had followed the truth are saved.

These are the main three pillars of 'belief' that all the Divine Prophets, from Adam to Mohammad and Easa and Moosa, with one intention and one voice preached to the people. Otherwise, for what other purpose had they come? To what had they promised people? And from what had they

---

[1] Holy Qor'aan: Soorah 21, Aayah 92.

warned people? The holy Qor'aan refers to the justification of the Day of Judgement and of the resurrection of the dead:

> *((AND HE STRIKES OUT A LIKENESS FOR US AND FORGETS HIS OWN CREATION. SAYS HE: WHO WILL GIVE LIFE TO THE BONES WHEN THEY ARE ROTTEN? SAY: HE WILL GIVE LIFE TO THEM WHO BROUGHT THEM INTO EXISTENCE AT FIRST, AND HE IS COGNISANT OF ALL CREATION[1].))*

> *((IS NOT HE WHO CREATED THE HEAVENS AND THE EARTH ABLE TO CREATE THE LIKE OF THEM? YEAH! AND HE IS THE CREATOR (OF ALL), THE KNOWER.*
> *HIS COMMAND, WHEN HE INTENDS ANYTHING, IS ONLY TO SAY TO IT: BE, SO IT IS[2].))*

2: MORALS

The holy religion of Islam commands from its followers sound morals and prohibits them from vile acts and cruelty. This method of commanding of virtues, as well as being compatible with man's logic, is also approved by all other divine religions, therefore, you will not find any virtues in the religion of Islam unless it has also appeared as a virtue in the laws of the religion of Easa, Moosa and the other prophets.

The root of all virtues falls back on to six principles:

1- Purity of the tongue
2- Purity of the ear
3- Purity of the eye
4- Purity of the heart

---

[1] Holy Qor'aan: Soorah 36, Aayah 78-79.
[2] Holy Qor'aan: Soorah 36, Aayah 81-82.

5- Purity of the stomach
6- Purity of the desires

    1. Purity of the tongue: from lies, gossip, slander, mockery, worthless talk, giving false testimony and issuing false orders, ...
    2. Purity of the ear: from listening to music, lies, gossip and any unjust and ugly talk and noises.
    3. Purity of the eye: from glancing upon things which are considered unlawful (haraam) to look at, such as (for men) to look at (non-Mahram) women...
    4. Purity of the heart: from grudges, jealousy, selfishness, hypocrisy, showing off, vanity...
    5. Purity of the stomach: from eating and drinking things that are religiously unlawful (haraam) such as eating of bacon, pork, (or any pig related meat) and drinking wine (or any other alcoholic drink), using drugs and consuming through unlawful earnings.[1]
    6. Purity of sensual desires: from anything that is not in line with chastity and modesty.

Can it be true that a prophet be sent for the people but yet he does not deter them from evil deeds and does not command of them decency? Would he allow for them contempt and insulting languages? Of course not! The prophets had all, with one objective and one voice, invited people towards righteousness and purity, to modesty and chastity, to perseverance and pleasantness, and to socialising.

---

[1] Food provided by money that has been obtained unlawfully is considered 'haraam'. (Translator).

The holy Qor'aan relays the words of the Prophet Easa:

((AND DUTIFUL TO MY MOTHER, AND HE HAS NOT MADE ME INSOLENT, UNBLESSED...[1])).

And from the words of Rasoolollaah[2]:

((AND MOST SURELY YOU CONFORM (YOURSELF) TO SUBLIME MORALITY[3].)).

3: WORSHIP

In all the Divine Messages there were calls for Salaat[4], Fast, Zakaat[5], Hajj[6], Jihad[7], Amr-Bil-Ma'roof[8], Nahi-Anil-Munkar[9], Tawalla[10] and Tabarra[11]. In the holy religion of Islam, these religious commandments, including 'khoms'[12] which is in the same category of zakaat, are known as Furoo-e-Deen (branches of religion). Not only have these commandments appeared in the numerous passages of the

---

[1] Holy Qor'aan: Soorah 19, Aayah 32.
[2] Rasoolollaah is a title given to prophet Mohammad by Allaah. It means: Messenger of Allaah.
[3] Holy Qor'aan: Soorah 68, Aayah 4.
[4] Prayer. (Translator).
[5] A kind of Islamic Tax. (Translator).
[6] Pilgrimage to Makkah. (Translator).
[7] To strive or fight in the way of God. (Translator).
[8] To enjoin what is right, inviting people to all that is good. (Translator).
[9] To forbid what is wrong, preventing people from doing bad. (Translator).
[10] Love and friendship with the good, i.e. love and respect the Ahl al-Bayt and to be friendly with their friends. (Translator).
[11] Disassociation with the bad, i.e. to disassociate or keep aloof from the enemies of Ahl al-Bayt. (Translator).
[12] A kind of Islamic Tax. (Translator).

divine Books, particularly of the holy Qor'aan as an order for us to act upon, but Man also commands others to these acts and every human character recognises them as sound morals.

Is performing salaat not one way of being thankful of God's bounties and of being submissive to His Splendour and Grandeur? Or can any intelligent person believe that God, with all His Mercy and Compassion for His beings, is unworthy of gratitude and submission?

Is fasting not an order for health and discipline? It benefits not only the person who keeps fast but the society as well. It purifies the body and the mind; once in a year the body's system begins to rest, the surplus fat that are stored in the body are burnt, it prevents excessive overweight, controls sensual desires, strengthens one's soul and self-control, it is a test of our sense of patience and endurance and it arouses such feelings of spirituality that one feels a certain closeness to God. Above all else, a person who keeps fast feels the pain of hunger and thus begins to think about those who are needy and less fortunate.

Is khoms and zakaat not the rightful payment by the wealthy for the good and the benefit of the society? One of the greatest benefits for the society is to ease the burden of poverty and to raise the quality of life by creating a security for the impoverished and the poor.

Is Hajj not a great Islamic congregation that each year draws crowds of people to the House of God[1], a House that God has placed as a focal point for the people, a place where they think of God and where they can focus upon improving and progressing their society, and a place where through their acts of worship they cleanse their hearts that have rusted as a result of their sins? And is it not where black and white, rich and poor, young and old, dressed in one colour with one heart

---

[1] Ka'bah 'House of God' is not meant as a house in which God lives but a site that was built by the order of God. (Translator).

and one voice, in the line of unity gather in one place and revive the soul of equality and brotherhood within themselves and demonstrate to the world the Islamic unity and friendship?

Is Jihad not an act of destroying corruption? Is it not about cleansing the world from the oppressors and brutality and of saving the oppressed from the claws of the dictatorship and colonisation? And is it not an act of breaking the chains of ignorance and ending the degradation caused by some vile and worthless tyrants?

Is Amr-Bil-Ma'roof and Nahi-Anil-Munkar not an order that is necessary for the overall welfare of a progressive society? If the reformists were no longer to exist would the earth and its inhabitants not be drawn towards corruption?

Does friendship with the righteous, and enmity with evil not account as an essential element for the advancement of a desirable society, so that people would embrace good values and turn away from evil and depravity?

It is on such basis that we see within progressive societies enormous respect and admiration that is held for their intellectuals and reformists but that for the corrupt and the ignorant they have only dislike and contempt.

These are the Islamic acts of worship and these prayers form the main foundation of every one of the divine religions, such that none of these acts are excluded from their divine laws.

The holy Qor'aan quotes the Prophet Easa:

((AND HE HAS MADE ME BLESSED WHEREVER I MAY BE, AND HE HAS ENJOINED ON ME PRAYER AND POOR-RATE SO LONG AS I LIVE[1].)).

And to the followers of Rasoolollaah[SAA][1] it says:

---
[1] Holy Qor'aan: Soorah 19, Aayah 31.

((O YOU WHO BELIEVE! FASTING IS PRESCRIBED FOR YOU, AS IT WAS PRESCRIBED FOR THOSE BEFORE YOU, SO THAT YOU MAY GUARD (AGAINST EVIL)[2].))

It has been narrated in ahaadeeth (narrations) that the Prophet Moosa performed the pilgrimage of Hajj and that the other prophets before him and those that came after him also performed the Hajj pilgrimage. The holy Qor'aan orders us to acts of worship in all its passages:

((...AND PILGRIMAGE TO THE HOUSE (HAJJ) IS INCUMBENT UPON MEN FOR THE SAKE OF ALLAAH, (UPON) EVERYONE WHO IS ABLE TO UNDERTAKE THE JOURNEY TO IT...[3]))

((AND FROM AMONG YOU THERE SHOULD BE A PARTY WHO INVITE TO GOOD AND ENJOIN WHAT IS RIGHT AND FORBID THE WRONG...[4]))

((GO FORTH LIGHT AND HEAVY, AND STRIVE HARD IN ALLAAH'S WAY WITH YOUR PROPERTY AND YOUR PERSONS[5].))

((MOHAMMAD IS THE APOSTLE OF ALLAAH, AND THOSE WITH HIM ARE FIRM OF HEART AGAINST THE UNBELIEVERS, COMPASSIONATE AMONG THEMSELVES...[6]))

---

[1] *Sallallaaho Alayhe wa Aalih* = May Allaah bliss him and his descendents.
[2] Holy Qor'aan: Soorah 2, Aayah 183.
[3] Holy Qor'aan: Soorah 3, Aayah 97.
[4] Holy Qor'aan: Soorah 3, Aayah 104.
[5] Holy Qor'aan: Soorah 9, Aayah 41.
[6] Holy Qor'aan: Soorah 48, Aayah 29.

((You shall not find a people who believe in Allaah and the latter day befriending those who act in opposition to Allaah and His Apostle...[1])).

((And when Ebraaheem and Ismail raised the foundations of the House (they said): Our Lord! Accept from us; surely Thou art the Hearing, the Knowing[2].)).

((...And We enjoined Ebraaheem and Ismail saying: Purify My House for those who visit (it) and those who abide (in it) for devotion and those who bow down (and) those who prostrate themselves[3].)).

The holy Qor'aan further emphasises that Islam, with all its acts and commandments, is the religion of all the prophets and whoever turns away from Islam has in fact turned away from the prophets because the divine laws of all the prophets stem from one root, even though some of their commandments appear to be slightly different, and this is because of the different era and the progression of mankind.

((And who forsakes the religion of Ebraaheem but he who make himself a fool...
When his Lord said to him, Be a Muslim, he said: I submit myself to the Lord of the worlds.
And the same did Ebraaheem enjoin on his sons and (so did) Ya'qoob. O my Sons! Surely Allaah has chosen for you (this) faith, therefore die not unless you are Muslims[4].)).

---

[1] Holy Qor'aan: Soorah 58, Aayah 22.
[2] Holy Qor'aan: Soorah 2, Aayah 127.
[3] Holy Qor'aan: Soorah 2, Aayah 125.
[4] Holy Qor'aan: Soorah 2, Aayah 130-132.

4: OTHER DEEDS...

For an organised and well structured society there must be certain laws that deal with issues such as business transactions, marriages, divorce and crime, as humans, by nature have a yearning for social involvement and its dealings, just as some have a tendency to commit crime.

The decline and the progression of a society is dependent upon the interaction of its people. The more undesirable the relationships become, the more that particular community heads towards a decline. Therefore, a healthy society is one whose regulations are based upon justice and a decadent society is one that is governed by cruelty and corruption and is overtaken by a high crime rate.

Like all other divine religions, Islam outlines the issues of social relationships so clearly and with such precision that it leaves no room for uncertainty so as not to misguide or deviate people. For Example, with regard to business transactions the holy Qor'aan states:

((...ALLAAH HAS ALLOWED TRADING AND FORBIDDEN USURY...[1])).

((O YOU WHO BELIEVE! DO NOT DEVOUR YOUR PROPERTY AMONG YOURSELVES FALSELY, EXCEPT THAT IT BE TRADING BY YOUR MUTUAL CONSENT...[2])).

With regards to loans, in which there can be betrayals the holy Qor'aan thus orders that:

---

[1] Holy Qor'aan: Soorah 2, Aayah 275.
[2] Holy Qor'aan: Soorah 4, Aayah 29.

((O YOU WHO BELIEVE! WHEN YOU DEAL WITH EACH OTHER IN CONTRACTING A DEBT FOR A FIXED TIME, THEN WRITE IT DOWN; AND LET A SCRIBE WRITE IT DOWN BETWEEN YOU WITH FAIRNESS; AND THE SCRIBE SHOULD NOT REFUSE TO WRITE AS ALLAAH HAS TAUGHT HIM, SO HE SHOULD WRITE; AND LET HIM WHO OWES THE DEBT DICTATE, AND HE SHOULD BE CAREFUL OF (HIS DUTY TO) ALLAAH, HIS LORD, AND NOT DIMINISH ANYTHING FROM IT; BUT IF HE WHO OWES THE DEBT IS UNSOUND IN UNDERSTANDING, OR WEAK, OR (IF) HE IS NOT ABLE TO DICTATE HIMSELF, LET HIS GUARDIAN DICTATE WITH FAIRNESS; AND CALL IN TO WITNESS AMONG YOUR MEN TWO WITNESSES; BUT IF THERE ARE NOT TWO MEN, THEN ONE MAN AND TWO WOMEN FOR AMONG THOSE WHOM YOU CHOOSE TO BE WITNESSES, SO THAT IF ONE OF THE TWO ERRS, THE SECOND OF THE TWO MAY REMIND THE OTHER... AND BE NOT AVERSE TO WRITING IT (WHETHER IT IS) SMALL OR LARGE, WITH THE TIME OF ITS FALLING DUE; THIS IS MORE EQUITABLE IN THE SIGHT OF ALLAAH AND ASSURES GREATER ACCURACY IN TESTIMONY, AND THE NEAREST (WAY) THAT YOU MAY NOT ENTERTAIN DOUBT (AFTERWARDS)...[1])).

Referring to the act of giving testimony the Qor'aan says:

((...AND DO NOT CONCEAL TESTIMONY, AND WHOEVER CONCEALS IT, HIS HEART IS SURELY SINFUL...[2])).

With regards to marriage:

---

[1] Holy Qor'aan: Soorah 2, Aayah 282.
[2] Holy Qor'aan: Soorah 2, Aayah 283.

((AND MARRY THOSE AMONG YOU WHO ARE SINGLE AND THOSE WHO ARE FIT AMONG YOUR MALE SLAVES AND YOUR FEMALE SLAVES; IF THEY ARE NEEDY, ALLAAH WILL MAKE THEM FREE FROM WANT OUT OF HIS GRACE...[1])).

((...THEN MARRY SUCH WOMEN AS SEEM GOOD TO YOU, TWO AND THREE AND FOUR; BUT IF YOU FEAR THAT YOU WILL NOT DO JUSTICE (BETWEEN THEM), THEN (MARRY) ONLY ONE...[2])). (4:3)

((AND WHEN YOU DIVORCE WOMEN AND THEY REACH THEIR PRESCRIBED TIME, THEN EITHER RETAIN THEM IN GOOD FELLOWSHIP OR SET THEM FREE WITH LIBERALITY, AND DO NOT RETAIN THEM FOR INJURY, SO THAT YOU EXCEED THE LIMITS, AND WHOEVER DOES THIS, HE INDEED IS UNJUST TO HIS OWN SOUL...[3])).

With regard to breast-feeding babies:

((AND THE MOTHERS SHOULD SUCKLE THEIR CHILDREN FOR TWO WHOLE YEARS FOR HIM WHO DESIRES TO MAKE COMPLETE THE TIME OF SUCKLING; AND THEIR MAINTENANCE AND THEIR CLOTHING MUST BE BORNE BY THE FATHER ACCORDING TO USAGE; NO SOUL SHALL HAVE IMPOSED UPON IT A DUTY BUT TO THE EXTENT OF ITS CAPACITY; NEITHER SHALL A MOTHER BE MADE TO SUFFER HARM ON ACCOUNT OF HER CHILD...[4])).

And on punishment and revenge:

---

[1] Holy Qor'aan: Soorah 24, Aayah 32.
[2] Holy Qor'aan: Soorah 4, Aayah 3.
[3] Holy Qor'aan: Soorah 2, Aayah 231.
[4] Holy Qor'aan: Soorah 2, Aayah 233.

((O YOU WHO BELIEVE! RETALIATION IS PRESCRIBED FOR YOU IN THE MATTER OF THE SLAIN; THE FREE FOR THE FREE, AND THE SLAVE FOR THE SLAVE, AND THE FEMALE FOR THE FEMALE, BUT IF ANY REMISSION IS MADE TO ANYONE BY HIS (AGGRIEVED) BROTHER, THEN PROSECUTION (FOR THE BLOODWIT[1]) SHOULD BE MADE...[2])).

((AND WE PRESCRIBED TO THEM IN IT (THE TAWRAAT) THAT LIFE IS FOR LIFE, AND EYE FOR EYE, AND NOSE FOR NOSE, AND EAR FOR EAR, AND TOOTH FOR TOOTH, AND (THAT THERE IS) REPRISAL IN WOUNDS; BUT HE WHO FORGOES IT, IT SHALL BE AN EXPIATION FOR HIM...[3])).

Referring to eating and drinking:

((O YOU WHO BELIEVE! INTOXICANTS AND GAMES OF CHANCE AND (SACRIFICING TO) STONES SET UP AND (DIVIDING BY) ARROWS ARE ONLY AN UNCLEANNESS, THE SATAN'S WORK; SHUN IT THEREFORE THAT YOU MAY BE SUCCESSFUL.
THE SATAN ONLY DESIRES TO CAUSE ENMITY AND HATRED TO SPRING IN YOUR MIDST BY MEANS OF INTOXICANTS AND GAMES OF CHANCE...[4])).

((...(WHO) ENJOINS THEM GOOD AND FORBIDS THEM EVIL, AND MAKES LAWFUL TO THEM THE GOOD THINGS AND MAKES UNLAWFUL TO THEM IMPURE THINGS...[5])).

((...EAT AND DRINK AND BE NOT EXTRAVAGANT...[1])).

---

[1] Blood money. (Translator).
[2] Holy Qor'aan: Soorah 2, Aayah 178.
[3] Holy Qor'aan: Soorah 5, Aayah 45.
[4] Holy Qor'aan: Soorah 5, Aayaat 90-91.
[5] Holy Qor'aan: Soorah 7, Aayah 157.

This is how Islam explains each one of its commandments and pays great attention to the welfare of the society. However, this is nothing new as all the other divine religions, from the time of the prophet Adam to this present time within which the last of the religious orders are from Rasoolollaah, endeavour to establish an organised society.

There are still many traces of other religions pertaining to the previous prophets, although they have been distorted and interfered with, and their divine truths have been made to appear as superstitions that only a few scattered pages of the original commandments can be found amongst the texts. It is therefore clear that there are no major differences between the divine religions except for very minor ones, and even these differences are not in the principle or the commandments of the religion but in the circumstances, the times and the environment of that particular period. For example, in the time of the Prophet Moosa, the Qeblah (the direction towards which the Muslims pray) was Bait-ul-Muqaddas (the present day Jerusalem) but in the time of Rasoolollaah, Ka'bah in Makkah became the direction of the Qeblah. This change was not because God had initially made a mistake but it was because in the time of the Prophet Moosa the population was low and Bait-ul-Muqaddas was considered as the capital and a cultivated land, but in the time of Rasoolollaah the countries expanded and the world population increased and Makkah became the centre of the world, hence the Qeblah was changed accordingly.

So these were the divine laws and religions and their divine commandments. Can you distinguish a difference between them?

---

[1] Holy Qor'aan: Soorah 7, Aayah 31.

((...AND IF IT WERE FROM ANY OTHER THAN ALLAAH, THEY WOULD HAVE FOUND IN IT MANY A DISCREPANCY[1].))

And in your opinion can the principle of the religions change so that it becomes possible for God to have a partner, or that the truth becomes ugly, or that to help the poor by means of zakaat becomes a bad deed? No! Never will this be!

---

[1] Holy Qor'aan: Soorah 4, Aayah 82.

THE LAST PROPHET

A human being goes through different stages in life: first he is an infant, then he grows up and becomes a youth, thus he heads for old age. Each of these phases demand certain necessities, i.e. for a child it is play and leisure, for youth and adulthood the necessity is pride and to work hard and for the old age it is contemplation and experiences. After old age there remains no other phase in life.

Knowledge and education also go through stages: school begins from the first grade until it reaches the last stages of university, it is therefore not appropriate to teach the 5th grade to someone who is either at a lower or a higher grade.

When we look back at the different phases of the human society we see that it is just like the life span of a person. When we look carefully at the previous religions and take into account their circumstances within the last centuries we can see clearly that these religions, as with education, had certain stages. Each nation required certain discipline and needed a religion that was suitable for their needs; and each religion had suited its time and its followers, although we realise that all the religions were one in principle but varied only in some of the particularities. Therefore, this variation within the religions is similar, for example, to mathematics which starts from the first grade and continues until the last stages of university; in every stage mathematics is being taught but the lessons of one grade are different to another grade, as they are in accordance with the level of individual understanding and the standard increases as the students' intellect develop.

The assigning of the prophets with regard to their call being public or private also differed with one another. The assignment of prophet Yoonos, as according to the holy Qor'aan *"WE SENT YOONOS TO 100,000 OR MORE PEOPLE"* was for this particular number of people. The prophet Loot was called upon the people of one particular city, as was the case with the prophets Saaleh, Hood and Sho'ayb (peace be upon them). The reason for this was that on one hand the nations were different from one another, and on the other hand different cities were far and apart and communication between them difficult, therefore assigning one messenger for all the nations was not practical. For this reason, there were two or more prophets at one time and each one was responsible for inviting his own people to religion.

In addition to this, the type of corruption that dwelled amongst one nation varied from that which eroded another nation, as a result each prophet was responsible for destroying the corruption from amongst his own nation.

Amongst all the prophets, whose numbers according to narrations totalled 124,000, there were only five who were universally assigned - for the west and the east of the world. These five were the Prophets Nooh, Ebraaheem, Moosa, Easa[1] and Mohammad because they had better resources and facilities to spread their teachings and also the laws and orders of their religion were of utmost perfection and themselves were more solid in strength and determination.

---

[1] Also: Jesus.

Perhaps it was for this reason that they were given the title of 'Ulel Azm' meaning the Arch-Prophets, the Resolute Ones.

As the nations were escalating towards development one messenger was not enough to drive them towards perfection, therefore new religious laws (*shari'ah*) were introduced to compliment and perfect the previous ones, although they were still based upon the skeleton of the previous laws. This is the same as when a student goes further up from one grade to the next, or that he completes year five and begins to study year six. He has to put aside all the text books of the previous year and obtain the new books but he has not discontinued with his studies and is still a student.

If we were to compare the nations that were in the time of the Prophets Nooh and Ebraaheem to those children with a junior school aptitude, and the nations of Moosa and Easa to those of senior school aptitude, and compare the nation of Mohammad to those youths who are ready to start a university education, we are not far from the truth. It may be that the words of Rasoolollaah[SAA][1] when he said: "I was surely sent to complete the noble characters" were aimed at this point. It is evident from this narration that the Divine Prophets revived the desirable characters within the people by their invigorating teachings and that Mohammad was the one to take this noble prophetic mission further into the peak of perfection.

Hence, this was the mystery of the prophetic mission of Mohammad, and this was the commonality of his religious laws with the other divine religions, and this was the merit of the religion of Mohammad over the other religions. The religion of Mohammad is the final stage for the advancement of man worldwide and because it holds the perfect methods

---

[1] *Sallallaaho Alayhe wa Aalih* = May Allaah bliss him and his descendents.

for advancement it is permanent and eternal.

Therefore, for as long as man is in existence the religious laws of Mohammad rule over people. The holy Qor'aan refers to his prophethood as being the last:

((...BUT HE (MOHAMMAD) IS THE APOSTLE OF ALLAAH AND THE LAST OF THE PROPHETS...[1])).

The holy Qor'aan refers to the religion of Islam:

((AND WHOEVER DESIRES A RELIGION OTHER THAN ISLAM, IT SHALL NOT BE ACCEPTED FROM HIM, AND IN THE HEREAFTER HE SHALL BE ONE OF THE LOSERS[2].)).

It is narrated that:

((The halaal[3] of Mohammad remains halal until the Day of Judgement and the haraam[4] of Mohammad remains haram until the Day of Judgement[5].)).

The human society will not gain total salvation and prosperity unless it follows the holy religion of Mohammad, accept the invigorating teachings of the Prophet wholeheartedly and benefit from its guidance and surrender to its commandments. The religion of Mohammad is detached from rigidity, superstitions and falsehood. It is a religion that is true and eternal.

In your opinion is it imaginable that a time will come when these Divine Commandments are no longer acceptable:

---

[1] Holy Qor'aan: Soorah 33, Aayah 40.

[2] Holy Qor'aan: Soorah 3, Aayah 85.

[3] All things that are allowed/lawful. (Translator).

[4] Opposite of 'halaal', things that are forbidden. (Translator).

[5] Basa'er al-Darajaat / al-Saffaar = page 148.

((SURELY ALLAAH ENJOINS THE DOING OF JUSTICE AND THE DOING OF GOOD (TO OTHERS) AND THE GIVING TO THE KINDRED, AND HE FORBIDS INDECENCY AND EVIL AND REBELLION...[1])).

((...AND HELP ONE ANOTHER IN GOODNESS AND PIETY, AND DO NOT HELP ONE ANOTHER IN SIN AND AGGRESSION...[2])).

((AND FROM AMONG YOU THERE SHOULD BE A PARTY WHO INVITE TO GOOD AND ENJOIN WHAT IS RIGHT AND FORBID THE WRONG[3].)).

((AND DO NOT MAKE YOUR HAND TO BE SHACKLED TO YOUR NECK NOR STRETCH IT FORTH TO THE UTMOST (LIMIT) OF ITS STRETCHING FORTH, LEST YOU SHOULD (AFTERWARDS) SIT DOWN BLAMED, STRIPPED OFF[4].)).[5]

((...AND THAT WHEN YOU JUDGE BETWEEN PEOPLE YOU JUDGE WITH JUSTICE[6].)).

---

[1] Holy Qor'aan: Soorah 16, Aayah 90.
[2] Holy Qor'aan: Soorah 5, Aayah 2.
[3] Holy Qor'aan: Soorah 3, Aayah 104.
[4] Holy Qor'aan: Soorah 17, Aayah 29.
[5] For a more clear understanding, this verse is referring to giving in the way of charity, i.e. do not give too little and do not give too much that is over your limit. (Translator).
[6] Holy Qor'aan: Soorah 4, Aayah 58.

PROOF OF PROPHETHOOD

A prophet is a representative of God on earth. If anyone was to claim to be of honourable status should people just take their word for it? Of course not, we would never acknowledge a doctor unless he/she possesses professional qualifications, or if someone were to claim to be an engineer we would accept their claim once they have produced their relevant qualifications.

How can we therefore believe a person, without a proof, when he claims to be a Messenger of the God of the entire universe Who holds the reins of life and death in His power? Unless he produces evidence that confirms he is a Messenger or a Prophet his claim will never be accepted. He must therefore produce a convincing argument to prove his claim, and such a proof of Prophethood is that God certifies his prophecy. And how is that certified? Do we see God? God cannot be seen. Do we hear His word? God does not speak to anyone. So what is the proof of Prophethood? The proof is that: The Prophet performs a supernatural act that no one but God is capable of doing. This is indeed the best proof because meddling with the laws of nature cannot be done by anyone except by one who is the deputy of the Creator of nature.

Every single prophet performed a supernatural act during his time that has brought man to his knees and one that no other person has ever been able to repeat, thus their prophetic missions were always successful. People would gather around them with such passion and excitement to follow their teachings and to wholeheartedly embrace the Divine commandments. Amongst the Prophets, Moosa[1] performed nine miracles: *"AND CERTAINLY WE GAVE MOOSA NINE CLEAR SIGNS[2]"*. One of the miracles was when he dropped his walking stick it turned into a serpent, his other miracles were that he would place his hand on his chest and when he brought his hand out it would shine like the sun. The holy Qor'aan says about the miracles of Moosa:

((AND SAYING: CAST DOWN YOU STAFF. SO WHEN HE SAW IT IN MOTION AS IF IT WERE A SERPENT, HE TURNED BACK RETREATING, AND DID NOT RETURN. O MOOSA! COME FORWARD AND FEAR NOT; SURELY YOU ARE OF THOSE WHO ARE SECURE.
ENTER YOUR HAND INTO THE OPENING OF YOUR BOSOM, IT WILL COME FORTH WHITE WITHOUT EVIL, AND DRAW YOUR HAND TO YOURSELF TO WARD OFF FEAR; SO THESE TWO SHALL BE TWO ARGUMENTS FROM YOUR LORD TO FERON[3] AND HIS CHIEFS, SURELY THEY ARE A TRANSGRESSING PEOPLE[4].))

Easa[5] the son of Maryam performed such miracles that no one ever doubted their authenticity: he brought back the sight of a blind man, cured the lepers, brought the dead back to life and he created birds out of mud ... The holy

---

[1] Also: Moses.
[2] Holy Qor'aan: Soorah 17, Aayah 101.
[3] The Pharaoh.
[4] Holy Qor'aan: Soorah 28, Aayaat 31-32.
[5] Also: Jesus.

Qor'aan says:

> *((WHEN THE ANGELS SAID: O MARYAM, SURELY ALLAAH GIVES YOU GOOD NEWS WITH A WORD FROM HIM (OF ONE) WHOSE NAME IS THE MESSIAH, EASA SON OF MARYAM, WORTHY OF REGARD IN THIS WORLD AND THE HEREAFTER AND OF THOSE WHO ARE MADE NEAR (TO ALLAAH)[1].))*

> *((AND HE WILL TEACH HIM THE BOOK AND THE WISDOM AND THE TAWRAAT[2] AND THE ENJEEL[3].*
> *AND (MAKE HIM) AN APOSTLE TO THE CHILDREN OF ISRAEL: THAT I HAVE COME TO YOU WITH A SIGN FROM YOUR LORD, THAT I DETERMINE FOR YOU OUT OF DUST LIKE THE FORM OF A BIRD, THEN I BREATH INTO IT AND IT BECOME A BIRD WITH ALLAAH'S PERMISSION AND I HEAL THE BLIND AND THE LEPROUS, AND BRING THE DEAD TO LIFE WITH ALLAAH'S PERMISSION AND I INFORM YOU OF WHAT YOU SHOULD EAT AND WHAT YOU SHOULD STORE IN YOUR HOUSES; MOST SURELY THERE IS SIGN IN THIS FOR YOU, IF YOU ARE BELIEVERS[4].))*

One of the miracles of the Prophet Ebraaheem was that he did not burn in the fire that was set up by the people belonging to the tribe of Nimrod. The holy Qor'aan describes it:

> *((WE SAID: O FIRE! BE A COMFORT AND PEACE TO EBRAAHEEM[5].))*

There were also the miracles of the other prophets

---

[1] Holy Qor'aan: Soorah 3, Aayah 45.
[2] The Holy Book of Moosa. (Translator).
[3] The New Testament. (Translator).
[4] Holy Qor'aan: Soorah 3, Aayah 48-49.
[5] Holy Qor'aan: Soorah 21, Aayah 69.

such as the camel of the Prophet Saaleh, the storm of the Prophet Nooh, etc... Every prophet performed a miracle that was appropriate for the circumstances at the time in order to prove a clear reasoning that was acceptable.

The Prophethood of Moosa was during a time in which sorcery and witchcraft were widespread and highly professional magicians were popular therefore, the Prophet performed the miracle of his walking stick and his hand and when those magicians witnessed his miracles they realised that his was not the art of witchcraft but a miracle that could not have been possible without the command of God, as a result they declared their faith in Moosa's God and prepared themselves for the torturous punishment of the Pharaoh that was to befall them.

During the time of the Prophet Easa, science was progressing and professional medicine men were emerging, so the Prophet Easa performed the miracles of curing the lepers and bringing back to life the dead and giving sight to the blind. Had it been the other way round where Moosa had introduced the miracles of Easa, the people of Moosa could claim that they knew nothing of medicine and that what he was performing was nothing but advanced medicine. Likewise, had Easa performed the miracles of Moosa his people could argue that they knew nothing of the tricks of magic and that he was merely a magician with advanced techniques. The Prophets' argument and reasoning could therefore not have been effective and the people would have had a viable excuse in disregarding them as Prophets.

The fact that there were people from the medical profession who had confessed to the miracles of Easa being far more superior than the power of medicine, and that there were highly skilled magicians who could not repeat what Moosa had performed, leaves no doubt that these acts were supernatural and beyond the capability of any human being.

They could only have been made possible by the command of God – the same God that the entire universe bows and surrenders to and the sky and the earth obey His command.

MOHAMMAD AND THE QOR'AAN

At a time when the light of knowledge had extinguished from amongst the Arab nations and in its place ignorance had spread over its people who lacked culture and education, the light of the Prophet of Islam: Mohammad (peace be upon him) shone through.

Within those circumstances how was the Prophet to prove to the people that he was a Messenger of God and that it was necessary for them to follow his teachings? The only solution was to bring forth something that people could relate to so that he could in turn, ask them to produce the same like it.

Knowledge and education at that time were only limited to gaining oratory and poetical skills and people favoured strongly the gatherings of such rhetorics and poetry. It was because of these gatherings that the public spent days assembling in the bazaars/markets, hence the famous story about the 'Bazaar of Akkaadh'...

Rasoolollaah[1] presented the Qor'aan and proclaimed to all of the Arabs to produce a book similar it, if they could.

---

[1] Rasoolollaah is a title given to prophet Mohammad by Allaah. It means Messenger of Allaah.

All the Arab orators came forth but failed. Once again, for the second time the Prophet asked them to produce two chapters similar to those of the Qor'aan, again they failed, and at the third call he asked them to at least produce, if they could, one chapter that could be similar to the smallest chapters of Qor'aan such as 'Tawheed' (Ch. 112) or 'Al-Kawthar' (Ch. 108). Again, the Arabs could not succeed. The holy Qor'aan refers to this incident:

> *((SAY: IF MEN AND JINN SHOULD COMBINE TOGETHER TO BRING THE LIKE OF THIS QOR'AAN, THEY COULD NOT BRING THE LIKE OF IT, THOUGH SOME OF THEM WERE AIDERS OF OTHERS[1].))*
>
> *((OR, DO THEY SAY: HE HAS FORGED IT. SAY: THEN BRING TEN FORGED CHAPTERS LIKE IT AND CALL UPON WHOM YOU CAN BESIDES ALLAAH, IF YOU ARE TRUTHFUL.*
> *BUT IF THEY DO NOT ANSWER YOU, THEN KNOW THAT IT (THE QOR'AAN) IS REVEALED BY ALLAAH'S KNOWLEDGE AND THAT THERE IS NO GOD BUT HE; WILL YOU THEN SUBMIT?[2]))*
>
> *((AND IF YOU ARE IN DOUBT AS TO THAT WHICH WE HAVE REVEALED TO OUR SERVANT, THEN PRODUCE A CHAPTER LIKE IT AND CALL ON YOUR WITNESSES BESIDES ALLAAH IF YOU ARE TRUTHFUL.*
> *BUT IF YOU DO (IT) NOT AND NEVER SHALL YOU DO (IT), THEN BE ON YOUR GUARD AGAINST THE FIRE OF WHICH MEN AND STONES ARE THE FUEL; IT IS PREPARED FOR THE UNBELIEVERS[3].))*

---

[1] Holy Qor'aan: Soorah 17, Aayah 88.
[2] Holy Qor'aan: Soorah 11, Aayaat 13-14.
[3] Holy Qor'aan: Soorah 2, Aayaat 23-24.

The miracle of Rasoolollaah was not only that of the Qor'aan. History has recorded many of his miracles but they were miracles that took place for that particular era. The Qor'aan however, is the everlasting miracle that shall remain, and in every sense, was and will always be the Supreme Book in the entire universe.

QOR'AAN AND THE DIVINE SCRIPTURE

God does not pass down anything except the truth and He will not command anything that is unjust. But, the enemies of humanity and those with a mind of ignorance mix the right with wrong and the truth with falsehood.

The Tawraat that was sent down to Prophet Moosa was a torch of guidance; the Enjeel (New Testament) that was revealed to Prophet Easa was perfect and ideal, but it was not long before the Jews and the Christians altered and distorted these two Divine Books. They added extracts that had originally not existed and deleted some of their original texts. It is recommended that the readers take a brief look at these two books, known as the Old and New Testaments or The Holy Book, in order to witness the alternations that are so evident and thereby confirm our claim.

Do you believe that the following verses are the words and the Divine revelations of the judicious God:

> "The Prophet Loot drank wine and lay with his first born and on the second night he drank wine and lay with his younger daughter" (Genesis 19:30-38)

Isaiah 20:2, 3 says that "the Lord spoke to Isaiah, saying go and loose the sackcloth from off thy loins, and put off thy shoe from thy foot. And he did so, walking naked and barefoot. And the Lord said, like as my servant Isaiah hath walked naked and barefoot for three years..."

Ezekiel 4:12,13 says that God ordered Ezekiel to bake bread with dung! "And thou (Ezekiel) shalt eat it as barley cakes, and thou shalt bake it with dung that cometh out of man, in their sight..."

Galatians 3:13 claims that Easa is accursed "Christ hath redeemed us from the curse of the law, *being made a curse for us*: for it is written, Curse is everyone that hangeth on a tree."

These are just a few of the superstitions that are too shameful to mention, such as God's wrestling match with some of His Prophets (Genesis 32:24), the adulterous actions of some of the Prophets, God walking in heaven or His descent to earth in order to separate the different races! (Genesis 3:7 and 11:1)

Could it truly be that a book which curses Easa and accuses Prophet Loot of adultery, or makes a mockery of the Messenger of God by claiming that they consumed human waste and walked around naked, is a Divine book of revelations sent by God for the guidance of man? Certainly not!

God has very appropriately stated in the verses of the Holy Qor'aan:

((BUT ON ACCOUNT OF THEIR BREAKING THEIR COVENANT WE CURSED THEM AND MADE THEIR HEARTS HARD; THEY ALTERED THE WORDS FROM THEIR PLACES

AND THEY NEGLECTED A PORTION OF WHAT THEY WERE REMINDED OF...
AND WITH THOSE WHO SAY, WE ARE CHRISTIANS, WE MADE A COVENANT, BUT THEY NEGLECTED A PORTION OF WHAT THEY WERE REMINDED OF...[1]*)).*

((WOE, THEN, TO THOSE WHO WRITE THE BOOK WITH THEIR HANDS AND THEN SAY: THIS IS FROM ALLAAH, SO THAT THEY MAY TAKE FOR IT A SMALL PRICE; THEREFORE WOE TO THEM FOR WHAT THEIR HANDS HAVE WRITTEN AND WOE TO THEM FOR WHAT THEY EARN[2]*.)).*

And these people are those to whom the holy Qor'aan has referred:

((THE LIKENESS OF THOSE WHO WERE CHARGED WITH THE TAWRAAT, THEN THEY DID NOT OBSERVE IT, IS AS THE LIKENESS OF THE ASS BEARING BOOKS, EVIL IS THE LIKENESS OF THE PEOPLE WHO REJECT THE COMMUNICATIONS OF ALLAAH; AND ALLAAH DOES NOT GUIDE THE UNJUST PEOPLE[3]*.)).*

The holy book (i.e. Old Testament/New Testament) is astonishing! Other historic and romantic novels rate far better. This divine book is like a history overwhelmed with superstitions and contradictions, it is filled with words that are meaningless and disturbing and which lacks intellectual significance and spirit. The Christian history proves that this book has been distorted and interfered with, not once or twice but many times over. Such is the state of a Divine Book!

---

[1] Holy Qor'aan: Soorah 5, Aayaat 13-14.
[2] Holy Qor'aan: Soorah 2, Aayah 79.
[3] Holy Qor'aan: Soorah 62, Aayah 5.

But the Holy Qor'aan is a Book in which nothing inappropriate appears. God has said about the Qor'aan:

((SURELY WE HAVE REVEALED THE REMINDER AND WE WILL MOST SURELY BE ITS GUARDIAN[1].)).

Within the Holy Qor'aan the eye witnesses the commandments, the knowledge and wisdom, the truth and justice, morals and etiquette, advice and guidance, righteousness and honesty, rhetoric and eloquence, society and civilisation, the beginning and the resurrection of man, the making of the creation, the world and the hereafter, heaven and hell, the stories regarding the Prophets narrated with the respect and purity that is befitting their title, the lives and the fate of the past nations, the lessons and experiences....

And why should the Qor'aan not be so, when it is God's words and messages; a revelation, a guidance, a divine radiance, and are the commands of the Creator to the creation, commands that all beings should obey until the last moments of life.

---

[1] Holy Qor'aan: Soorah 15, Aayah 9.

PART IV:
IMAAMAH (THE SUCCESSORSHIP OF THE PROPHET)

THE IMAAM

- Who is a leader?
- What qualities does he possess?
- What are his signs?

The above questions need to be considered and contemplated upon but we shall first explain them briefly and then in detail.

1. An Imaam is the deputy and a successor of the prophet with respect to all the duties that related to the prophet, such as: removing or appointing a ruler, governing and leadership, safeguarding the religious beliefs of an Islamic country, spreading the religious commandments. The only difference is that the prophet gained his knowledge directly from God but an Imaam acquires his knowledge from the prophet.
2. The qualities of a prophet, which were mentioned before, are also visible in an Imaam, therefore, a prophet and an Imaam possess the following traits: A perfect knowledge, piety, courage,

generosity, righteousness, a noble character, a pleasing countenance, a pure soul, infallibility, enthusiasm, their speech should match their character, total obligation to religious orders...

3- An Imaam must be appointed by the prophet who is acting upon the orders of God.

4- There are many signs of recognising an Imaam but the most obvious one is that he is the best amongst the people of his time and that no one matches or possesses any of his qualities, therefore, a model for a perfect human within that era is only him whilst others are all imperfect. Also, just as with the prophets, an Imaam performs extraordinary acts and miracles in order to prove that he has been assigned by God as a leader and deputy.

These are the main factors relating to an Imaam or leader of an Islamic nation. Each one of these holds certain discussions and principles, which will be pointed at briefly.

WHO ARE THE IMAAMS?

The A'emmah whom the holy Prophet has appointed are twelve and they are:

	Imaam's Name	Title	Nickname
1	Ali Ibn Abi Taalib	Ameer al-Mo'meneen[1]	Abu al-Hasan
2	Hasan Ibn Ali[2]	Mojtaba	Abu Mohammad
3	Hosayn Ibn Ali	Sayyed al-Shohada'[3]	Abu Abdollah
4	Ali Ibn al-Hosayn	Zayn al-Aabedeen	Abu Mohammad
5	Mohammad Ibn Ali	Baaqir-ul-Uloom	Abu Ja'far
6	Ja'far Ibn Mohammad	Saadiq	Abu Abdollah
7	Moosa Ibn Ja'far	Kaadhem	Abu al-Hasan
8	Ali Ibn Moosa	Redhaa	Abu al-Hasan
9	Mohammad Ibn Ali	Jawaad	Abu Ja'far
10	Ali Ibn Mohammad	Haadi	Abu al-Hasan

---

[1] A title given to Imaam Ali, the first Caliph, by Allaah. It means: Commander of the Faithful. (Translator).
[2] 'Ibn' means son, therefore Ibn Ali refers to him being the son of Ali. (Translator).
[3] Means: Master of the Martyrs.

11	Hasan Ibn Ali	Askari	Abu Mohammad
12	Mahdi (Mohammad)	Saaheb al-Zamaan	Abu al-Qaasem

The first Imaam is Ameer al-Mo'meneen[(AS)1] who is the cousin of the holy Prophet and also his son-in-law and the rest of the A'emmah are the children of Ameer al-Mo'meneen from the father's side and are the children of the Prophet through their mother Faatimah.

And Faatimah (peace be upon her) is the daughter of the holy Prophet and the wife of Ameer al-Mo'meneen and this great honourable lady possesses the same virtues as the A'emmah, except that according to narrations, she is considered even more superior than eleven of the A'emmah.

---

[1] *Alayhes Salaam* = Peace be upon him.

THE HISTORY OF AHL AL-BAYT[1]

The dates of the births and martyrdoms of the A'emmah[2], as well as the cause of their martyrdoms and the names of their assassins are as follows:

	Date of Birth	Date of Death	Cause	Assassin
1st Imaam	23 BH[3]	40 H	Sword	Ibn Moljam Moraadi
2nd Imaam	3 H	50 H	Poison	Jo'dah. By the order of Mo'aweyah
3rd Imaam	4th H	61 H	Sword	Shimr Ibn Theljawshan. By the order of Yazeed
4th Imaam	38 H	98 H	Poison	By the order of Ebraaheem Ibn al-Waleed
5th Imaam	58 H	117 H	Poison	By the order of Waleed Ibn

---

[1] Ahl al-Bayt means the 'People of the House' i.e. belonging to the household of the Prophet, his progeny, being the holy A'emmah. (Translator).
[2] Plural of Imaam.
[3] Before Hejrah. Hejrah is the migration of Rasoolollaah from Makkah to Madinah. It is also the beginning of the Moslem calandar.

				Abdolmalik
6th Imaam	80 H	148 H	Poison	Mansoor Dawaaneeqi
7th Imaam	128 H	182 H	Poison	Haaroon Abbaasi
8th Imaam	148 H	203 H	Poison	Ma'moon Abbaasi
9th Imaam	195 H	220 H	Poison	Mo'tasam Abbaasi
10th Imaam	214 H	254 H	Poison	Motawakkil Abbaasi
11th Imaam	232 H	260 H	Poison	Mo'tamad Abbaasi

The twelfths Imaam was born in the year 256 H. He is still alive and in occultation and shall reappear upon the command of God. He will bring universal justice after the world is empowered by oppression and injustices. We pray that the Almighty God hastens his reappearance and to place us as one of his followers.

WHAT QUALITIES DOES AN IMAAM POSSESS?

If we were to describe all the qualities of an Imaam in one small sentence and say that an Imaam is one who is the best leader of his time', our description still remains to be inadequate. It should instead be said that 'amongst all the people of the universe (upon whom it is obligatory to follow an Imaam) there does not exist a person who can surpass the qualities of an Imaam.

An Imaam is a representative of God and a deputy of the Messenger of God, therefore, how could it be that God and the Prophet assign for themselves a representative whilst a better person could be found amongst the nation? When an ordinary person wishes to select for himself a deputy who will continue with his affairs, he will most surely select the best and the most competent person, so imagine when it is God, the most Wise and Learned, and His glorious Prophet choosing such a deputy. Just as the Prophet has to be the most superior person than others, an Imaam must also be the best person amongst the nation because when it comes to leadership and guidance there is no difference between a Prophet and an Imaam.

Do you believe, for example, that if a minister of education were to recruit a principal for a school, he would choose someone who is less educated than the students, when he could in fact find a person of great excellence? Would anyone believe, therefore, God or His Prophet to be less thoughtful than an educational minister? Never will God and the Prophet exceed this intellectual and common law, therefore, selecting the most virtuous of people is vital for two reasons, (1) that whenever possible, one should rely upon their intelligence and follow a leader who is the best and the most outstanding of people, and (2) it is inappropriate to give a person of inferior character precedence over someone with perfect qualities. How can an intelligent mind allow someone who has a vile and a low character to be the leader and a guide of a righteous person?

The following verses of the holy Qor'aan refer to this point:

((SAY: IS THERE ANY OF YOUR ASSOCIATES WHO GUIDES TO THE TRUTH? SAY: ALLAAH GUIDES TO THE TRUTH. IS HE THEN WHO GUIDES TO THE TRUTH MORE WORTHY TO BE FOLLOWED, OR HE WHO HIMSELF DOES NOT GO ARIGHT UNLESS HE IS GUIDED? WHAT THEN IS THE MATTER WITH YOU; HOW DO YOU JUDGE?[1]))

((...ARE THOSE WHO KNOW AND THOSE WHO DO NOT KNOW ALIKE?...[2]))

((AND THEIR PROPHET SAID TO THEM: SURELY ALLAAH HAS RAISED TAALOOT TO BE A KING OVER YOU. THEY SAID: "HOW CAN HE HOLD KINGSHIP OVER US WHILE WE HAVE A GREATER RIGHT TO KINGSHIP THAN HE, AND HE HAS NOT BEEN GRANTED AN ABUNDANCE OF

---

[1] Holy Qor'aan: Soorah 10, Aayah 35.
[2] Holy Qor'aan: Soorah 39, Aayah 9.

WEALTH? HE SAID: SURELY ALLAAH HAS CHOSEN HIM IN PREFERENCE TO YOU, AND HE HAS INCREASED HIM ABUNDANTLY IN KNOWLEDGE AND PHYSIQUE[1].))

In his description of an Imaam, Imaam Redhaa[AS] said: "He is a scholar in whom there is no ignorance, a leader who is not weaker than any of his peers. God graces the prophets and the A'emmah and favours them with His wealth of knowledge and wisdom." In another narration, Imaam Redhaa[AS] also said: "An Imaam possesses certain qualities; he is the most knowledgeable, the most persevering, and the most pious of people.

THE ESMAH[2] OF AN IMAAM

One of the best qualities that must be evident in both an Imaam and a prophet is Esmah or immunity from sins. The strength of Esmah protects the prophet and the Imaam from committing any kind of sin or disobeying God however small or great, be it intentionally or by mistake. But this purity does not exceed the limitations of self-control where a Prophet or an Imaam is compelled not to commit sins. They therefore can commit sins but by self-control and of their own will power they choose not to disobey God. These people are so perfect in their religion that they would never consider neglecting God as much as a blink of an eyelid in case they commit a wrongdoing. They are like a sane person who would never blind himself by his own hands or cut his own throat... or better still, they are like a loving mother who

---

[1] Holy Qor'aan: Soorah 2, Aayah 247.

[2] Esmah is a state in which a person does not commit sins, does not make mistakes, does not forget, etc. Such a person is called: "Ma'soom", plural: "Ma'soomeen". All the prophets and their caliphs were Ma'soom. (Translator).

has the power to harm her own child but would never do so. These examples are only meant to draw the mind closer to the point, otherwise the status of the prophet and that of an Imaam are far greater than all that has been mentioned here.

WHY IS ESMAH NECESSARY FOR A PROPHET AND AN IMAAM?

If the representatives of God were not chaste or immune from sins and errors people would not have totally trusted them, and as a result, their belief in the authenticity of the Divine Laws would have faded. This lack of trust would also have been used as an excuse to disobey or disregard the Divine Commandments and as such, the prophets and the A'emmah could no longer accomplish their role of leadership.

It is also inappropriate that God would assign the affairs of the people to someone who is not immune from wrongdoings or who could alter the Divine laws as and when he wishes to, when it is in fact only God, the Creator of mankind, who can alter the laws that are set for mankind. God has the power to select someone who would neither deliberately nor mistakenly or absent-mindedly commit any wrongdoings. The holy Qor'aan talks about the Prophet:

> *((NOR DOES HE SPEAK OUT OF DESIRE.*
> *IT IS NAUGHT BUT REVELATION THAT IS REVEALED[1].))*.

> *((WE WILL MAKE YOU RECITE SO YOU SHALL NOT FORGET.*
> *EXCEPT WHAT ALLAAH PLEASES[2].))*.

---

[1] Holy Qor'aan: Soorah 53, Aayaat 3-4.
[2] Holy Qor'aan: Soorah 87, Aayaat 6-7.

The 'exception' that is in this verse 'except what Allaah pleases', does not mean that the Prophet would at times forget, but the fact that forgetfulness does not happen to the Prophet is by the will of God. Do not think that this is beyond the capability of God; in fact God is capable of making the Prophet suffer from absent-mindedness just like the ordinary people.

In describing the Prophet and the A'emmah the holy Qor'aan says:

((...ALLAAH ONLY DESIRES TO KEEP AWAY THE UNCLEANNESS FROM YOU, O PEOPLE OF THE HOUSE! AND TO PURIFY YOU A (THOROUGH) PURIFYING[1].)).

Imaam Saadiq[AS] had said that:

((The Prophets and their deputies are without sins as they are the pure ones who are immune from sins[2].)).

And Imaam Ali[AS] also said:

((One must only obey the Almighty God and His Messengers and those charged with authority – the A'emmah, and obedience of those charged with authority is vital as they are pure from sins and will not guide people to disobedience of God[3].)).

It has been narrated from Ibn Abbaas, who had said:

---

[1] Holy Qor'aan: Soorah 33, Aayah 33.
[2] Al-Khesaal / al-Sadooq = page 608.
[3] Elal al-Shara'e' / al-Sadooq = page 123.

((I heard the holy Prophet say: 'I, Ali, Hasan and Hosayn and nine others from the progeny of Hosayn are immune and safe from sins[1].))

Hosayn al-Ashqar narrates that he once asked Heshaam Ibn Hakam:

((The fact that you (Shi'as) claim that 'none other but a Ma'soom can be an Imaam', what does this Esmah mean?" Heshaam then referred this question to Imaam Saadiq[AS] who replied: "A Ma'soom is one who is under the protection of God from all sins, as Allaah says: 'WHOEVER HOLDS FAST TO ALLAAH, HE INDEED IS GUIDED TO THE RIGHT PATH[2] '[3].))

---

[1] Oyoon Akhbaar al-Redhaa / al-Sadooq = vol. 1, page 64.
[2] Holy Qor'aan: Soorah 3, Aayah 101.
[3] Ma'aani al-Akhbaar / al-Sadooq = page 132.

WHO APPOINTS THE IMAAM

As explained before an Imaam should possess all the qualities of perfection one of which is Esmah. Esmah is a hidden quality which no one but God is aware of, because an innocent appearance of a person is not sufficient proof of their purity as there were those who had outwardly appeared to be good people but later happened to be very evil or those people who were first considered to be honest but they turned out to be deceitful.

For example, in the case of Bal'am, who was considered one of the most pious of men to an extent that he was granted one of the grand names of Allaah, but after some time he strayed and joined the rank of the sinners and the ill fated. His story has been narrated in the following Qor'aanic verse:

((AND RECITE TO THEM THE NARRATIVE OF HIM TO WHOM WE GIVE OUR COMMUNICATIONS, BUT HE WITHDRAWS HIMSELF FROM THEM, SO THE SHAYTAAN OVERTAKES HIM, SO HE IS OF THOSE WHO GO ASTRAY. AND IF WE HAD PLEASED, WE WOULD CERTAINLY HAVE EXALTED HIM THEREBY; BUT HE CLUNG TO THE EARTH AND FOLLOWED HIS LOW DESIRE, SO HIS PARABLE IS AS

THE PARABLE OF THE DOG; IF YOU ATTACK HIM HE LOLLS OUT HIS TONGUE; AND IF YOU LEAVE HIM ALONE HE LOLLS OUT HIS TONGUE; THIS IS THE PARABLE OF THE PEOPLE WHO REJECT OUR COMMUNICATIONS...[1])).

Was it not Prophet Moosa, who is one of the Prophets of 'Ulel Azm' (the Grand Prophets), when he chose 70 people whom he had considered to be amongst the most pious of the entire nation of the Israelites, but these chosen ones later became non-believers and abandoned their religion? The holy Qor'aan refers to this incidence of Moosa and his followers as such:

((AND MOOSA CHOSE OUT OF HIS PEOPLE SEVENTY MEN FOR OUR APPOINTMENT; SO WHEN THE EARTHQUAKE OVERTOOK THEM...[2])).

And in another verse God explains the reason for their punishment:

((AND WHEN YOU SAID: O MOOSA! WE WILL NOT BELIEVE IN YOU UNTIL WE SEE ALLAAH MANIFESTLY, SO THE PUNISHMENT OVERTOOK YOU WHILE YOU LOOKED ON.
THEN WE RAISED YOU UP AFTER YOUR DEATH THAT YOU MAY GIVE THANKS[3].)).

Some of the Moslems claim that the Prophet of Islam never appointed anyone to succeed him but this claim is false and unjustified because, as we will point out later, the incidence of the Prophet appointing his successor has been

---

[1] Holy Qor'aan: Soorah 7, Aayaat 175-176.
[2] Holy Qor'aan: Soorah 7, Aayah 155.
[3] Holy Qor'aan: Soorah 2, Aayaat 55-56.

proved and there are numerous narrations that are acknowledged by all sects which relay the events.

There is an interesting narration of Imaam Redhaa[AS] when he addressed a person who was denying the issue regarding the Prophet's successor:

> ((Imaam Redhaa[AS] asked the scholar Ibn Raameen: Did the Holy Prophet not appoint himself a deputy when he left Madinah?
> Ibn Raameen: Yes, he appointed Ali.
> Imaam Redhaa: So, why did the Prophet not ask the people of Madinah select someone from amongst yourselves as you are not the sort of people who would turn to disobedience and be led astray?
> Ibn Daayen: Because the Prophet feared that there may be disagreement and conflict amongst the people.
> Imaam Redhaa: So? What would it have mattered, even if there were to be trouble the Prophet would have rectified them upon his return to Madinah?
> Ibn Dayen: Undoubtedly, the decision of the Prophet to appoint a deputy himself was the most appropriate.
> Imaam Redhaa: Therefore, did he appoint anyone to succeed him after his death?
> Ibn Dayen: No.
> Imaam Redhaa: Was the death of the Prophet not more important than his trip? His trip was for a short time, and this one was long and forever, so how was it that at the time of his death he was confident about the people whilst for a short journey of just a few days he was not, even

though he could have later rectified any troubles?[1])).

The Prophet of Islam proclaimed the Imaam and his successor many times. The first time was on the day when he gathered his relatives and he invited them to good morals and then appointed his successor. This event has been narrated by Tabari, Ibn Abil Hadeed and other historians:

Imaam Ali[AS] narrates that:

((When the verse 'AND WARN YOUR NEAREST RELATIVES' (26:214) was revealed to the Prophet, he said: 'Ali! Allaah has instructed me to invite my relatives to Islam; I became saddened by this order because I know that they would pay no heed but Gabriel came to me and conveyed: 'O Mohammad! If you do not perform this task your Lord will indeed punish you!' Ali! Prepare some food for us with a leg of mutton and some milk, then gather the sons of Abdul Mottalib so that I speak to them and pass on the Divine Message.' I did whatever the Prophet requested of me and invited the whole family.

The Prophet thus addressed his family: 'O the sons of Abdul Mottalib! I swear that amongst the whole nation I know of no Arab youth who brings you better than what I bring you. I bring for you the good of this world and of the Hereafter; my Lord has commanded me to summon you to the religion of Islam. Who amongst you will aid me in my mission so that after me he will be my legatee and my successor?' Ali[AS] said that: "Those present at the gathering turned their faces away from the Prophet, but I cried out 'It is I, O the

---

[1] Behaar al-Anwaar / al-Majlesi = vol. 23, page 75.

> *Messenger of God! In your mission I shall be your aid' the Prophet put his arms around me and declared: 'this man is my brother and legatee and my successor amongst you. Obey him, follow him and pay heed to his words[1].)).*

And the last time that the Holy Prophet reintroduced his successor was in the day of Eid of Ghadeer, an event which has been relayed by successive witnesses and narrations and we recount it here just as Tabari had:

> *((When the Holy Prophet was returning from the Farewell Pilgrimage they arrived at Ghadeer Khom. It was in the burning midday sun and the Prophet ordered the crowd of pilgrims to halt and announced for the prayers to be performed in congregation. After we had all gathered he began to deliver his address: 'Allaah has revealed this verse to me 'O APOSTLE! DELIVER WHAT HAS BEEN REVEALED TO YOU FROM YOUR LORD; AND IF YOU DO IT NOT, THEN YOU HAVE NOT DELIVERED HIS MESSAGE, AND ALLAAH WILL PROTECT YOU FROM THE PEOPLE' (5:67) The Angel Gabriel has brought me the command that I should stop at this place and to declare to every black and white person that Ali Ibn Abu Taalib is my brother and after me will be my legatee and successor and will be your Imaam.*
> *I had asked Gabriel for Allaah to excuse me from this task, as I know that the pious people are in the minority and that my enemies and tormentors are many but my Lord would not allow it unless I carry out my mission. O people! Know that God has assigned Ali for you as your guardian and*

---

[1] Shawaahed al-Tanzeel / al-Hasakaani = vol. 1, page 485.

leader and has made obedience of him obligatory upon everyone, his command is to be obeyed, and his speech is penetrating, whoever disobeys him is cursed and whoever follows him beholds the mercy of Allaah, listen and obey that Allaah is your Guardian and Ali is the deputy of Allaah and your leader and from then until the Day of Judgement the Caliphate amongst my children will be from the progeny of Ali...)).

As well as these two events there were many other occasions in which the succession of the Holy Prophet was firmly and clearly repeated and Islamic historians have narrated them.

On the day that the Holy Prophet was to depart this world he decided to write on paper of the leadership of Ali$^{(AS)}$ and reconfirm him as his successor and Caliph so that there does not arise any disputes after his death. But unfortunately, he was prevented from doing so. The Holy Prophet not only stipulated the leadership and the Caliphate of Ali$^{(AS)}$, he also introduced the other future A'emmah by their names one by one. Termethi narrates in his book the 'hadeeth' of Jaabir Ibn Samrah who recalls:

((THE HOLY PROPHET SAID: 'THE LEADERS OF THE RELIGION AFTER ME ARE TWELVE' THEN HE UTTERED SOMETHING VERY QUIETLY WHICH I COULD NOT HEAR SO I ASKED THE PERSON WHO WAS SITTING NEXT TO ME AND HE REPLIED: 'HE (THE PROPHET) SAYS THAT THEY ARE ALL FROM THE TRIBE OF QORASHI'[1].)).

Thereafter, every Imaam explicitly proclaimed the next Imaam that was to succeed him; Imaam Ali appointed Imaam Hasan, who then appointed Imaam Hosayn, who

---
[1] Behaar al-Anwaar / al-Majlesi = vol. 36, page 23.

appointed Imaam Zayn al-Aabedeen who appointed Imaam Baaqir who appointed Imaam Saadiq, who appointed Imaam Kaadhem, who appointed Imaam Redhaa, who appointed Imaam Jawaad who appointed Imaam Haadi and he appointed Imaam Askari who proclaimed Imaam of our time, Imaam Mahdi[AS]. Anyone who wishes to discuss or pursue this fact can refer to the narrations in the books of both, the Shi'as and the Sunnis.

In addition to their explicit affirmations, these A'emmah were each the most knowledgeable, devout, pious and chaste people and had more than any other person possessed the best of qualities, and had more than any other person distanced themselves from the world. Although they were not opposed to hard work and drive but at the same time they were not accumulating wealth and even shared their own daily earnings with the poor.

It is evident for all the Moslems that these qualities and features are only exclusively confined to the holy A'emmah and logic commands one to follow those who are greater and more superior.

THE IMAAM IN OCCULTATION

It is a human habit to deny the things that one cannot perceive. If people were not to realise the mistakes they make in many things then, to a certain extent, they could have a justified excuse but the fact that every day they become aware of one or two of their errors or wrongdoings their excuse can no longer be acceptable.

- A long time ago, the holy Qor'aan reported about the journeys of the Prophet Solaymaan on his flying carpet when he spent every other month travelling. But only those religious ones believed it, whereas some open-minded intellectuals dismissed it as superstitious! It was not until the last century when aeroplanes and space missiles ripped through the skies and roared into space that these intellectuals were astonished and thereby could no longer justify their denials regarding the incident of Prophet Solaymaan.

- A long time ago, the holy Qor'aan informed people about the eternity of the soul but those who were influenced by western beliefs claimed this to be a distorted idea of the Moslems and claimed that such beliefs were old tales, until science discovered the existence of soul and thus began to explore the world of souls and spirits. It was then that those who initially dismissed the idea bowed their heads to the glory and the magnificence of the Qor'aan.

- A long time ago, the holy Qor'aan had told us that the Prophet Nooh lived amongst his people for nine hundred and fifty years and propagated his religion. Again, some intellectuals dismissed it and claimed that it was against nature and totally impossible, until recently the medical science has found the answer for a longer life and the scientists believe that research into the longevity of life will be resolved in the near future. Again, those who disbelieved the idea confessed to the truthfulness of the Qor'aan.

And now, if these intellectuals are told that: according to narrations of the Holy Prophet and the A'emmah, the promised Imaam, Mahdi[AS] who was born in the year 256 H and is still alive until such time that God sees appropriate to reappear him; and that upon his reappearance he will fill and restore the world that is overtaken by cruelty and oppression, with justice, then they would claim that this cannot be possible… They would say that such belief is ancient superstitious and stems from the oppressed and fanatical societies of the past.

The existence of Imaam Mahdi[AS] is an undeniable truth, this Imaam will soon reappear and he will infiltrate the world with justice, despite the fact that some believe his existence to be superstitious and laugh at this idea.

As we mentioned earlier this is a human habit. No matter how inferior man's intellect and how limited his knowledge is, he remains pretentious and this in fact is a sign of foolishness and ignorance. Yet, on the other hand, we see those people who increase their knowledge and intellect but become more humble.

Socrates, the philosopher, was on his deathbed when he was asked what he had learnt throughout his life and from his experiences. He replied: "I have learnt that I know nothing!"

Yet, the youth of today claims that he knows all about the earth, the universe and its climate and that he has the knowledge of all the mysteries and the sciences of the world, that he knows the differences of body and soul, the beauty and the ugly. In fact, he boasts that the key to the secrets of the entire universe lies in his hand!!

The reappearance of the Divine Promise, Imaam Mahdi[AS] is something that even the Sunnis have narrated from the Holy Prophet in many of their books. Also, the Shi'ah sources have produced numerous narrations that the Holy Prophet and the A'emmah have passed down to us, the numbers of which are unaccountable.

You may refer to the books of 'Al Mahdi' by the late Ayatollah Sadr or 'Al Ghadeer' by Alameh Amini to gain more information.

PART V:
RESURRECTION

BODY AND SOUL

Everyone has two aspects, body and soul. Intelligence, comprehension of the soul, work and activity relate to the body. The body is like a garment that dresses the soul, therefore, it is the soul that sees, hears, tastes, touches, smells and thinks. Body is like a tool, just as a carpenter cannot saw the wood without a tool and it is the carpenter that cuts the wood not the tool, and the same as when a mechanic cannot design an engine without the appropriate equipment but in true fact the maker of the engine is the mechanic and not that equipment. Likewise, it is the soul that functions and not the body, the body is nothing more than a vehicle and a tool.

In addition to the five visible senses mentioned, the soul performs other functions such as thinking and comprehension. The truth about the soul is not clear, although we know of its existence but with all the advances science has made it is still not hopeful of discovering the mysteries of the soul. The holy Qor'aan refers to the mystery of the soul in the following verse:

((AND THEY ASK YOU ABOUT SOUL. SAY: THE SOUL IS ONE OF THE COMMANDS OF MY LORD, AND YOU ARE NOT GIVEN OUGHT OF KNOWLEDGE BUT A LITTLE[1].))

The materialists, in their own world of ignorance believe that after substance nothing else remains and they regard soul as one of the products of substance. They think that with such beliefs they could free themselves from the tangles of religion but the knowledge in recalling the soul, which was amongst one of the most popular scientific discoveries, has taken the blindfolds off their ignorance and their distorted beliefs.

When science was initially progressing into the existence of soul, the materialists tried to make a mockery of it and attempted to silence the scientists but their efforts were not effective until recently they bowed to the truth. The media and the laboratories tried with all their powers to destroy such a discovery to the extent that millions of people believed them. But it was not long before many books were written about the existence of the soul and today this belief is prevalent in most countries.

Soul does exist and just like a government that runs a country, it manages the system of our body. Soul is extensive and with regard to motion and stability it is not limited like the body. At times it even travels to far away cities and countries and sees many wonderful things, with the body of its owner still comfortably sleep in bed. Dreaming is nothing but a reflection of the extensive world of soul, and until now science has been unable to also discover the truth about dreaming.

The reason that some people deny the existence of the soul is either one of these two:

---

[1] Holy Qor'aan: Soorah 17, Aayah 85.

1- Ignorance and lack of knowledge on the subject
2- Escape from those things that lead to the belief in the existence of the soul

These two are like diseases that must be fought just as it is necessary to fight off malaria or an infection. Ignorance for us is an unforgivable sin, particularly since the West has surrendered to this truth which was initially our belief, and it was they who, after having denied this truth for over a century or two, decided to introduce it into their universities and scientific centres.

If one was to deny the truth, one has undoubtedly misguided himself from which he cannot escape unscathed and he will certainly suffer the consequences. He is like a person who denies the heat of the fire and with such a belief he throws himself into the fire; or like one who does not believe that poison can kill but when he takes it, it does kill him. Therefore, it is necessary for every individual to use their intellect so that they do not cause their own destruction through ignorance and by surrendering to their desires. If our proof for the existence of soul was based only upon the testaments of the prophets and their successors, it could be possible to accept the argument of those who deny the existence of soul and believe only in the senses but in today's world the issue of the soul falls into the same category as senses and this has been unfolded by many scientists and experiments.

On these bases, those who dismiss the existence of the soul have no grounds for their scepticism.

THE WORLD OF BARZAKH

Man encounters many phases on far and long journeys:

The body of man travels from earth into the world of plantation and (after consumption) turns into a sperm. The sperm travels into the womb where it is first a blood clot, then a small piece of flesh and after it develops bones and flesh it emerges as a complete human.

Again, he travels. He steps into this world as a newborn, he then becomes a child, then a youth and eventually grows old. Once more man's body returns to earth and after some time becomes dust. These are the stages of the journey of man's body.

As for the journey of man's spirit: According to the Islamic narrations, man's soul was created before his body and when he is an embryo the soul enters his body and remains with him until it is separated at death. The soul does not perish after death, on the contrary, it remains just as it was. If the person was a righteous person he will remain happy and joyful after death and if he was not he will suffer pain and torment. This period for the soul is called 'the world of Barzakh'. Barzakh means 'middle', in a sense that it is in the middle of the two worlds, the world that we currently live in, and the eternal world (the hereafter).

Fortunately, as we explained before, the science and the knowledge in the reappearance of the spirit has lifted the mystery surrounding the soul and has discovered amazing things which affirms all that the holy Qor'aan and the prophets said about the soul many centuries ago. As the holy Qor'aan says:

> *((AND DO NOT SPEAK OF THOSE WHO ARE SLAIN IN ALLAAH'S WAY AS DEAD; NAY, (THEY ARE) ALIVE BUT YOU DO NOT PERCEIVE[1].))*

> *((AND RECKON NOT THOSE WHO ARE KILLED IN ALLAAH'S WAY AS DEAD; NAY, THEY ARE ALIVE (AND) ARE PROVIDED SUSTENANCE FROM THEIR LORD.*
> *REJOICING IN WHAT ALLAAH HAS GIVEN THEM OUT OF HIS GRACE, AND THEY REJOICE FOR THE SAKE OF THOSE WHO, (BEING LEFT) BEHIND THEM, HAVE NOT YET JOINED THEM, THAT THEY SHALL HAVE NO FEAR, NOR SHALL THEY GRIEVE.*
> *THEY REJOICE ON ACCOUNT OF FAVOUR FROM ALLAAH AND (HIS) GRACE, AND THAT ALLAAH WILL NOT WASTE THE REWARD OF THE BELIEVERS[2].))*

A person once asked Imaam Ja'far Saadiq[AS][3]:

> *((After the soul is separated from the body, does it perish? The Imaam replied: No, rather, the soul remains[4].))*

---

[1] Holy Qor'aan: Soorah 2, Aayah 154.
[2] Holy Qor'aan: Soorah 3, Aayaat 169-171.
[3] *Alayhes Salaam* = Peace be upon him.
[4] Al-Ehtejaaj / al-Tabarsi = page 350.

Habbah Arani narrates that:

((It was near the afternoon when I went out of town with Ameer al-Mo'meneen, Imaam Ali$^{(AS)}$. His Highness stopped at the cemetery and he seemed as though he was chatting to his close friends. As his Highness was standing I, too was standing until I became tired then I sat down. I got tired of sitting and stoop up again for a while and as before, grew tired and sat down but again, I got tired and stood up and gathered my cloak and thus told him: "O' Ameer al-Mo'meneen, how long have you been standing, I feel bad for you, why not rest for a while." I then spread my cloak so that his Highness could sit on it. But the Imaam replied: 'Oh, Habbah! All this that you saw was a chat and a greeting with just one Believer." I asked him: "Do the spirits meet and chat as we do?" and he replied to me: "Yes, if the veil was to be lifted off your eyes you would be able to see that they are sitting in friendly groups and chatting." I asked again: "Do they have a body or are they just spirits?" He replied: "They are spirit"[1].))

Those scientists who have acquired knowledge in the existence of the soul say that they asked a spirit that they had summoned "Are you happy in the world in which you are or are you uncomfortable?" The spirit replied: "The spirits have different conditions and various levels." And they asked again: "Does there exist water, trees, gardens and buildings?" The spirit replied: "They do exist but much better and more beautiful than in the world but they are not like the ones that

---

[1] Al-Kaafi / al-Kolayni = vol. 3, page 243. Behaar al-Anwaar / al-Majlesi = vol. 6, page 267.

were seen in the world, rather like something that man has never seen."

Ever since that science has brought us the truth by means of experiments and experiences, no one can any longer claim that:

1- We do not meet our rewards of good and bad or see the angels, the heavenly palaces, gardens and the flowers; or ask
2- Who has brought us news from the other world so that we could accept it.

Scientific knowledge of the spirits answers these two questions as such:

1- We have seen the rewards of good and bad
2- The spirits have been recalled and they brought us news from that world.

THE ETERNAL LIFE

The Prophets had always promised the bounties of the next world to those people with good deeds and had warned the bad people of the fears of the next world; a world in which a grand court of justice will take place and where the good will receive their rewards and the bad will meet their punishment.

The materialists had always denied this fact and from the time that man was placed on earth, until the present time, there has always been conflict between the two groups and their followers. Their denials (of the next world) are based on the following reasons:

1- that they have never seen the dead to come back to life after burial;
2- they have not seen the 'other' world; and that
3- the soul perishes after death and therefore, its return is impossible.

This reasoning is similar to the ones used by those whom, until the discovery of America, had denied its existence, or similar to those who would not accept that a time will come when a person will be able to speak from the East and be heard at the same time by those in the West.

These justifications and reasonings are baseless and bear no substance. They are not even worthy of debate but in response to them it could be said that:

> 1- Many people have seen the dead come back to life such as the Prophet Ebraaheem and those who were present during the prophethood of Easa, so what different is there between this part of the history, which we all believe in, and the news about the next world?
> 2- And 3- Many people have seen the next world and due to the advanced scientific skills in recalling the spirits, they have told us about it. Also, the Prophets and the A'emmah had always told us about the next world.

Let us imagine that the world is to God just what a laboratory table is to a chemical scientist. The scientist uses the laboratory to put together the scattered parts of some minerals, and then separates the different parts, with the exception that the knowledge and the power of God is much greater than that of the scientist.

God has mentioned the denial of the non-believers in many Qor'aanic verses and He responds to them as such:

((AND SAYS MAN: WHAT! WHEN I AM DEAD SHALL I TRULY BE BROUGHT FORTH ALIVE?
DOES NOT MAN REMEMBER THAT WE CREATED HIM BEFORE, WHEN HE WAS NOTHING?[1])).

---

[1] Holy Qor'aan: Soorah 19, Aayaat 66-67.

Was man not at first made of dust, which turned into plant and then became an animal, then a sperm and then a human? The One that had initially the power to create has also the power to bring man back to life. As God says in the holy Qor'aan:

((WERE WE THEN FATIGUED WITH THE FIRST CREATION? YET ARE THEY IN DOUBT WITH REGARD TO A NEW CREATION[1].))

Indeed not! God will never falter in a new creation and in reviving the dead back to life.

((...AND YOU SEE THE EARTH STERILE LAND, BUT WHEN WE SEND DOWN ON IT THE WATER, IT STIRS AND SWELLS AND BRINGS FORTH OF EVERY KIND A BEAUTIFUL HERBAGE.
THIS IS BECAUSE ALLAAH IS THE TRUTH AND BECAUSE HE GIVES LIFE TO THE DEAD AND BECAUSE HE HAS POWER OVER ALL THINGS.
AND BECAUSE THE HOUR IS COMING, THERE IS NO DOUBT ABOUT IT; AND BECAUSE ALLAAH SHALL RISE UP THOSE WHO ARE IN THE GRAVES[2].))

A seed has no life, the soil is also lifeless so who is it that gives life to this seed in the darkness of the earth until it brings forth from each plant a beautiful set? Is it not God? And what difference is there between bringing to life a dead person and a dead seed?

((AND CERTAINLY YOU KNOW THE FIRST GROWTH, WHY DO YOU NOT THEN MIND?[3]))

---

[1] Holy Qor'aan: Soorah 50, Aayah 15.
[2] Holy Qor'aan: Soorah 22, Aayaat 5-7.
[3] Holy Qor'aan: Soorah 56, Aayah 62.

It has been narrated that a person presented himself to the holy Prophet with the intention of condemning him. He held a rotten bone and crumbled it in front of the holy Prophet whilst asking him: "Who is able to revive this crumbled bone?" In response to him the following verse was revealed:

> ((AND HE STRIKES OUT A LIKENESS FOR US AND FORGETS HIS OWN CREATION. SAYS HE: WHO WILL GIVE LIFE TO THE BONES WHEN THEY ARE ROTTEN? SAY: HE WILL GIVE LIFE TO THEM WHO BROUGHT THEM INTO EXISTENCE AT FIRST AND HE IS COGNIZANT OF ALL CREATION[1].)).

In any case, is it justifiable for some of the world's powerful figures to create corruption and commit murders and atrocities then die as great men with honour and glory, and yet they are not to be held responsible for all their crimes and atrocities! Is it not far from justice that those righteous people who have suffered for their decency and were persecuted by the oppressors do not meet their reward?

Absolutely not! God has placed the next world as the eternal world, the place for the rewards and the punishments of mankind. The holy Qor'aan says:

> ((SO, HE WHO HAS DONE AN ATOM'S WEIGHT OF GOOD SHALL SEE IT.
> AND HE WHO HAS DONE AN ATOM'S WEIGHT OF EVIL SHALL SEE IT[2].)).

---

[1] Holy Qor'aan: Soorah 36, Aayaat 78-79.
[2] Holy Qor'aan: Soorah 99, Aayaat 7-8.

HEAVEN AND HELL

Within this world for every thing that man does, from good or bad, ugly or pleasant, he will be reckoned with in the Day of Judgement. For every person there are guardian angels assigned to record all his deeds, be it blinking, listening, talking, touching or even inner intentions, etc. As the holy Qor'aan says:

> ((AND WE HAVE MADE EVERYMAN'S ACTIONS TO CLING TO HIS NECK, AND WE WILL BRING FORTH TO HIM ON THE RESURRECTION DAY A BOOK WHICH HE WILL FIND WIDE OPEN.
> READ YOUR BOOK; YOUR OWN SELF IS SUFFICIENT AS A RECKONER AGAINST YOU THIS DAY[1].))

And the moment the person's book of deeds is given to him, he says:

> ((AND THE BOOK SHALL BE PLACED, THEN YOU WILL SEE THE GUILTY FEARING FROM WHAT IS IN IT, AND THEY WILL SAY: AH! WOE TO US! WHAT A BOOK IS THIS! IT DOES NOT OMIT A SMALL ONE NOR A GREAT

---

[1] Holy Qor'aan: Soorah 17, Aayaat 13-14.

ONE, BUT NUMBERS THEM (ALL); AND WHAT THEY HAD DONE THEY SHALL FIND PRESENT (THERE); AND YOUR LORD DOES NOT DEAL UNJUSTLY WITH ANYONE[1].))

*((SO, HE WHO HAS DONE AN ATOM'S WEIGHT OF GOOD SHALL SEE IT.
AND HE WHO HAS DONE AN ATOM'S WEIGHT OF EVIL SHALL SEE IT[2].))*

*((AND AT THE TIME WHEN THE HOUR SHALL COME, AT THAT TIME THEY SHALL BECOME SEPARATED ONE FROM THE OTHER.
THEN AS TO THOSE WHO BELIEVED AND DID GOOD, THEY SHALL BE MADE HAPPY IN A GARDEN.
AND AS TO THOSE WHO DISBELIEVED AND REJECTED OUR COMMUNICATIONS AND THE MEETING OF THE HEREAFTER, THESE SHALL BE BROUGHT OVER TO THE CHASTISEMENT[3].))*

There exists in that world of heaven many bounties: the black-eyed houris (the nymphs of paradise), the young men with eternal youth that are like fresh pearls, fruits in abundance, all varieties of drink, and every kind of food one desires but, better than all these, there is the satisfaction and the pleasure of God. Friends sit around each other on their thrones; their countenance is formed with the joys and the pleasures of the heavenly bounties. The prayer of those in heaven is: "Lord, you are indeed pure and sacred" and their greeting is 'Salaam'[4]. They do not suffer the cold or the heat, neither death nor old age. There appears for them whatever they wish for and desire and they remain within this eternal

---

[1] Holy Qor'aan: Soorah 18, Aayah 49.
[2] Holy Qor'aan: Soorah 99, Aayaat 7-8.
[3] Holy Qor'aan: Soorah 30, Aayaat 14-16.
[4] Meaning 'peace'. (Translator).

place forever happy and blissful. God cuts out the root of jealousy and malice out of their hearts. They feel no jealousy towards each other, nor do they hold grudges.

But in the world just opposite the eternal heaven there is the eternal hell, with its intense fire. Its inhabitants are fed with germs and dirt and with the bitterest infernal food. Their drink is sizzling hot and their hands and feet are locked in chains. They wish for their death every second and some send curses on others, blaming each other for their sins. The clothes that they wear are of tar and they live in the depth of the fire. But worse than this, there is the wrath of God. They have no support and can find no friend or companion. There is no refuge or escape and death approaches them from all directions yet they do not die, instead, they reside in this eternal torment for ever. They do not die so as not to be relieved of their torment and yet they do not live as an ordinary healthy people...

The heaven with all its bounties is the reward for the Believers and the righteous people with good deeds who had surrendered to the Divine Commands.

The hell, with all its torments and punishments is for the non-Believers who abandoned religion and lived a life in the rank of the wrongdoers.

Throughout our educational years at school, college and university we put ourselves through difficulties and hardship so that we could eventually obtain a diploma, a degree or a doctorate in order that we spend the remainder of our living days, possibly another 50 years maximum, in comfort and security, even though the life in this world comes with a lot of difficulties, sufferings, pain, sorrows and hardship. A businessman works hard, suffers, spends sleepless nights, and strives hard so that he could stash away some money for a secure future and to remain safe from poverty. Say, after a while he succeeds, then grief, sorrow and problems befall him from all sides and just like everyone else he begins to suffer pain and old age… In that case, why do we not begin to do the simple things in our short life so that in the eternal life we can obtain an ever-lasting rest and peace that is unimaginable and bears no limits, and in which there exists no discomforts?

Let us imagine that everything that all the Prophets had preached, the Divine Book guided us to, and the great personalities of the world have faith in, and the accounts of the witnesses and the experiences of the spirits have proved, are all suspicious and we remain sceptical. But, is that *probability* not enough?

And even if all these news were not true, what had we lost? Imaam Saadiq told Ibn Abil Awjaa':

> *((If what you say is correct, that there is no judgement and reckoning, and we are wrong, then neither of us has lost anything; but if what you claim is untrue and we are right, then we will have gained eternal life in the heaven and you will have lost it!))*.

There is a piece of Arabic poetry by Ameer al-Mo'meneen which, when translated, he says:

"The astrologer and the medicine man both said: 'the dead will not be brought back to life', but I tell you that if your words are true I will not suffer but if my words are true, then you will both suffer."

Mohammad Ibn Mahdi Hosayni Shirazi